I0461400

SPARKS FROM LIGHTNING BUGS

AND OTHER LIFE LESSONS

RICHARD HOWERTON

Sparks from Lightning Bugs and Other Life Lessons

Richard Howerton

Cover design by Jake Dilley
Digital artwork by Rob Howerton
Interior layout by Emily Ruf
Produced by Spoonbridge Press

Copyright © 2022 Richard T. Howerton, III

All rights reserved. No part of this book may be reproduced in any manner without the express written consent of the author, except in the case of brief excerpts in reviews and articles.

First U.S. Edition, 2022

Print ISBN: 979-8-9866588-0-3
Ebook ISBN: 979-8-9866588-1-0

Printed in the U.S.A.

To my family, especially my soul mate, Janice, who lived with me through these events and their direct developmental and repercussive impacts upon me and our family.

Special thanks to my mother and father, who, from 1959 to 1967, took their family of five to forty-eight states and twelve foreign countries, most nights of which we spent in a canvas tent. Those experiences created many adventures and instilled in me a love of travel that eventually birthed a quarter of the stories written here.

CONTENTS

CONTENTS

CONTENTS

CONTENTS

CONTENTS

CONTENTS

INTRODUCTION

When I was a kid, time stood still on Sunday mornings when I was trapped in a church pew, listening to a sermon. That my father was the preacher made no difference. My wool trousers came alive and clawed at my thighs. The hook of my clip-on tie dug at my throat as if it were drilling for blood. The hand on my mother's reliable Bulova watch seemed stuck. I thought time might pass if I counted the blue feathers in the lady's hat in front of me. I attempted self-hypnosis by staring into the beady black eyes of the mink perched on her shoulders and biting its own tail. I prayed that God would bless me with another fly to land on my hand so I could sense the tickle of its slight feet as they jerked and paused, traversing the lines of my palm.

But every time, just when my restlessness reached its zenith and I was certain boredom would kill me, something happened: Dad told a story. No matter how tortured I felt during my capture, when Dad launched into a tale, I paid attention. And so did everyone else.

Time after time, when fidgetiness infected the congregants, causing them to change the position of their crossed knees, search their bulletins for the next act, or fake a cough to stay awake, Dad, as if he perceived our mutual distress, would pause his theological arguments and tell a story about human beings. We perked up, sat still, and listened. He brought us back. It was an immense talent of his and a gift to us. Dad called them "sermon illustrations," but even then, I knew what they really were: stories.

I have been intrigued by the power of stories ever since. Stories can make points, teach us important life lessons, bring us closer together, warm our hearts, make us laugh, mist our eyes, or move us to sheer wonder as we wander the pathways of life. They help us remember the good times and give us solace through the bad.

Stories can even change the way our brains work. Neuroscientists have shown through brain scans of speakers and listeners that the same areas of their brains "light up" with activity when they hear an engaging story.[1] That a powerful story can get people on the same wavelength has long been considered common sense, but now, neuroscience has shown it occurring in real time on functional MRI scans.

Most of all, stories connect us. Many times, when I reconnect with an acquaintance, the first thing they recall about our shared time together is a story, one that I either told or played an active role in myself.

The vignettes that follow are all true stories that I have shared with family, friends, and colleagues throughout my life. The events occurred when I was a child, a teenager, a young man, a husband, and a father, and throughout my health care executive career. They've taken place all

---

1 Wendy A. Suzuki et al., "Dialogues: The Science and Power of Storytelling," *The Journal of Neuroscience* 38, no. 44 (August 10, 2010): 9468–9470.

over the country and in various locations around this great world. (Consult the appendix at the end for a list of stories in each of these locations.)

When reading or listening to a story, we create mental images; like snowflakes, each image is unique. The digital art on the cover are the creations of my youngest son, Rob, wielding his computer animation art to convey what his mind saw in a few of my stories. Your mind will birth your creations.

These stories touch on themes that most of us can relate to or deal with at one point. You'll find stories about the ups and downs of family life. ("Outrunning a Storm" and "Your Son Is Fine, But . . ." are especially revelatory.) You'll read stories of responsibility, both in and out of the workplace. ("County Cuts" and "The Power Outage" are examples of what happens when we embrace our responsibilities, however difficult; "The Colossus of Another Rhodes" and "The Elizabeth River" are stories about stepping up and taking charge as needed.) Some stories touch on faith ("My Dream within a Dream"; "Bible Convention"), others on race ("Dixie" and "Lexington Revisited"). Several stories examine how simple misunderstandings can lead to unexpected misadventures (such as "The Great Walls of China"). Still others touch on the joy of new beginnings ("Intoxicant Love"; "Follow Your Bliss"), the grief of loss ("Dad's Illness: Part V"; "This Life and One More"), and the stories we share along the way ("Mom to a Grown-up Me"). And of course, if you're looking for a moment of humor in this thing we call life, you might want to try "DMV Photo," "Moon Tag," "Are You James Ford?" or many others throughout this book. (If you're in a particular mood, a second appendix in the back lists stories arranged under broad themes.)

At the end of each story throughout this book, I will offer a few lessons that I took away from the event. But as you read them, remember, that's what I got out of it. The same story can convey different life lessons to different people, sometimes even to the same person. Some of the lessons you'll encounter may even contradict each other. What can I say? That's life.

Stories make us human. Family stories become a part of our inheritance, and likewise, stories that we share with family and friends live on.

Everyone has a story. As you read mine, remember: there's never a better time for you to begin sharing yours.

Richard Howerton
August 2021

SPARKS FROM LIGHTNING BUGS

AND OTHER LIFE LESSONS

SPARKS FROM LIGHTNING BUGS

One evening in the summer of 1968, when I was seventeen, I decided to drive the long way home.

Alone, I saw a movie in Roanoke. Heading back to Blacksburg at the foot of Christiansburg Mountain, I shunned the lanes of US 460 and turned instead toward the valleys that cradled meandering strips of asphalt laid over what were once likely Indian trails.

The night sky was clear and black with no moon. I always loved this road with no constraining lines. I held its every turn, dip, and straightaway locked in my memory, and best of all, tonight, I had it to myself. Through my lowered windows wafted aromas of honeysuckle and newly mown hay. My AM radio blasted alternating thumps of soul and soaring psychedelic rifts, propelling my mood to a new height of euphoria.

In the middle of a sweeping right turn around the edge of a wooded hill, I saw something out of my left periphery in what I knew should be an empty meadow. *Is that light? How could that be?* I slowed and glanced toward whatever it was, and when I saw it, I slammed on my brakes and killed the headlights.

About a hundred feet away stood a solitary tree, twinkling. It was a massive oak, the sort of solo tree a farmer leaves in a field for unknown reasons, and it was pulsating with the blinks of thousands of lightning bugs—fireflies, some call them—covering every surface with a blanket of illumination like nothing I had ever seen.

I sat there in slack-jawed awe and let the power of creation settle over me. The serendipity of my having chosen this route began to sink in, and with it, an epiphany of divine purposefulness descended upon me. I was meant to be here in this place and at this time. This was an amazing gift that I was meant to share with others.

It was then a certain young woman crossed my mind.

After snapping a mental picture to mark this spot, I headed home to call the girl-of-my-dreams-of-the-week. She answered the phone and said yes, she would go to a movie with me in Roanoke for three nights hence—a miracle in and of itself on any other night. But on this night of miracles, I would have been surprised if she had said no.

◆ ◆ ◆

Our date night was a duplicate of the one three nights before: dark, clear, and gorgeous. After the movie, she didn't object to my suggestion that we take the scenic valley road home. All was going according to plan, I thought as I tried to steady my breathing and keep my palms dry. Then, my reckoning alerted me that the magic spot was approaching.

When I slowed down, she asked nervously, "Why are you stopping?"

"Just wait. You are about to witness the most amazing thing you've ever seen."

I stopped the car, turned off the lights and the radio, pointed over my left shoulder, and announced more than asked, "See what I mean?"

"What exactly am I supposed to see?"

I jerked around and saw nothing but the occasional blink of a solitary lightning bug here and there, no more than you might see during a neighborhood game of badminton at dusk. For a hopeful second, I prayed I was in the wrong spot. Then the dark silhouette of the oak tree in its empty field told me otherwise.

I tried to explain. No amount of eloquence, no description nor elucidation, made any difference. My night ended a few minutes later with a stolen kiss on a frosty cheek.

I have driven that road to that exact spot many nights since, and I never saw that tree full of lightning bugs again.

Life Lessons
- Some opportunities just can't be shared.
- Timing is everything.

DO YOU SEE ANY WILDLIFE?

It was a perfect day for hiking the paths of the Norris Geyser Basin in Yellowstone National Park. The sky, with a blue found only in the West, hosted scattered white clouds above the vast views on the horizon.

I walked hand in hand with my four-year-old son, Rob, making sure he didn't dash off from the walkway to see more bubbles emerging through the earth's brittle crust out of thermal springs below. My wife, Janice, walked with Seth and Drew, our other two sons, somewhere up ahead.

I'd longed for this kind of day while planning our "Out West" adventure. Five days of driving across nine states had delivered us here to this place of glory and wonder. It occurred to me that this was the perfect moment to ask for the umpteenth time, "Do you see any wildlife?"

This, of course, elicited groans from my captive audience, just as my father's repetitive questions had from his family and me on our cross-country trips years ago. Now, with the wisdom of age, I understood. There could be a golden marmot in the sage or a mule deer peeking out of trees somewhere or, better yet, buffaloes on the hills in the distance below those spectral clouds. It always pays to keep an eye out.

"Rob, do you see any wildlife?"

"Sure, Dad. There's a snake."

I looked down and saw Rob's sneaker about to land near the head of a dark snake.

I screamed. Rob screamed. The snake screamed. Then, a four-foot garter snake slithered into the brush.

Life Lessons

· If you are constantly looking toward the future, you will miss the present.

· Gazing into the horizon is great as long as someone is watching the path.

I DIDN'T EVEN KNOW YOU WERE PREGNANT!

My Labor Day escape with my first two sons—a trip to the mall skating rink—was a gift of silence and respite to nine-months-pregnant Janice. We were expecting our third son to arrive any week now. When we left, Janice said, "Don't you go and break a leg!"

I had grown up in Blacksburg back when the Virginia Tech duck ponds froze so frequently that both Western Auto and Blacksburg Hardware kept racks of ice skates in stock. I grew up skating on those ponds where town and gown would gather to cut figure eights or play hockey, tag, and crack the whip. At night under strings of white lights, island campfires stoked flirtatious courtships and fond memories.

When our neighbor Glenn Mease and his kids picked us up, I was proud to tote my own skates so I could shun the dull blades that the Charlotte mall rented. On the ice, I was quick to zip front and back, executing quick double-blade stops that showered ice on my wide-eyed sons.

Then, just when I felt seventeen again, I made one cut too far. My feet shot up toward the roof, and when I landed on the small of my back, my skull whiplashed into the ice. There was only a little blood, but within minutes, I confessed to Glenn that I couldn't remember how I had gotten there. He took me to the hospital.

I was told later that in the emergency room of Presbyterian Hospital—where I served on the executive administrative staff—the nurses chuckled when I kept repeating, "I used to be a good skater. I used to be a good skater."

When Janice came alongside my gurney, she cooed her concern. When she leaned over to kiss me, her expansive belly pressed into my arm. When I felt our baby kick, I was surprised and asked, "What's that?"

"Why, that's our baby," Janice answered, looking at me with her beautiful blue eyes.

"Baby?" I said, starting to cry. "I didn't even know you were pregnant!"

That's when things got serious—CTs, MRIs, a night in the hospital for inpatient observation.

Though I returned to work in two days, I knew I still wasn't right. Our third son, Rob, was born a week later, on September 11, 1988. I was present for the birth, but I slept through most of it in the labor room lounge chair. Exhaustion oppressed me, and I slept double my normal hours. I questioned my ability, terrified that my incompetence would cost me my job and my ability to support our family.

I decided to fake it. But through the self-doubt that haunted me, I felt increasingly trapped. I couldn't recall things I'd just learned. "It will come to me" became my hopeful mantra to my diminished short-term memory. When well-wishing coworkers asked how I was doing, I got angry and said, "You'll have to tell me! How should

I know?" My immune system was off, and I caught every cold and virus that came along. I tried to camouflage my executive inabilities with platitudes and inertia. I was sure "they" would find me out. I felt myself spiraling downward into an abyss of failure.

I don't remember when suicide became a logical option for me. I just remember believing that if I ever admitted to anyone that I was having such thoughts, my career would be over.

◆ ◆ ◆

One morning, our kind medical librarian asked what she could do to help. I knew that if I gave her something to do, she would leave me alone, so I asked her to research whether there was a connection between concussions and immune function. A few days later, she bounded in with printouts from medical libraries around the world, thanks to a new "information superhighway." She had found something called "post-concussion syndrome," a condition that could linger for months, but she cautioned that most of the research came from the Soviet Union and Eastern Europe.

I thanked her and began reading, and I found that this syndrome could be responsible for all my symptoms. That there was a possible explanation for my condition thrilled me.

A few weeks later, I told my internist about the research our medical librarian had found and asked if he had ever heard of post-concussion syndrome. He said that he had.

"Why didn't you tell me?" I asked. I didn't say what my mind was screaming: I wish you had told me—I was thinking about the best way to commit suicide! If only I had known!

"Because," he said, "it only occurs ten to twenty percent of the time. I didn't want to plant that seed in your mind. It was a judgment call." Then he added, "You seem to be doing better. Right?"

He was right. Six months later, I had begun to recover. But it took over a year before I felt like I was finally well. Ever since my skating accident, my short-term recall remains somewhat diminished. But thankfully, I can recall long-term memories; otherwise, I wouldn't have been able to write this book or recall the stories that have meant so much to me throughout my life.

Life Lessons

· Just because you used to be good at something doesn't mean you can always pick it up where you left off.

· Make sure that your skill exceeds your desire to show off. (And take care of your head—thoughts and memories are precious!)

HOLE IN THE WATER

In my grandmother Ora's pool one afternoon a few years into my adolescence, I was being a jerk to my two sisters, pinching them underwater and surprising them with facial splashes and full-body dunks. Ora kept watch over us, ensuring we didn't disappear into the murky green depths of her unfiltered, rectangular cement pond fed by natural spring water.

Ora called my name. My grandmother was a mountain woman of few words, and when she summoned someone, she was not meant to be trifled with. I climbed up the nearest ladder and scurried over to stand before her.

She stopped snapping the half runner beans that she had splayed out on a newspaper in her lap and looked straight at me. "Richard," she said, "you think you are so important? Just look over your shoulder and see how long it took for your hole in the water to fill in."

She threw the half runner in her hand into a steel pot of water. It made a tiny splash before settling among the mess of broken beans. Then she lowered her eyes from mine and picked up another.

Life Lessons
- Your time in the pool is your opportunity to determine how you will be remembered.
- If you leave the team, another player will fill the gap and carry on.

PUSSY WILLOW CONFESSION

For show-and-tell at Mrs. Allen's kindergarten, a classmate brought several branches of pussy willows.

Fascinating things those almond-sized gray tufts were, so much so that later that morning, my friend Kurt and I sneaked a private look at them. To our touch, the pussy willow flowers felt like velvet on the bare skin of our arms and faces. Wondering what they smelled like, I sniffed one. But in my excitement, I inhaled so fully that a single catkin broke off and flew up my nostril. There, it embedded itself so securely that it remained unmoved by all my subsequent snorts and puffs.

"Promise you won't tell!" I implored my wingman as if our conspiracy of silence would reverse my predicament. He promised, and he didn't. Nor did I.

By midmorning, sinus excruciation forced me to confess my plight and plead for mercy. My parents were called, and off we went to the doctor, who wrestled the pussy willow out of my nose with tongs that my mind still sees as a foot long.

◆ ◆ ◆

Postscript: At a recent high school reunion, my conspirator in this tale, who is now a professor of music and a trombone master at a small liberal arts college in the upper Midwest, greeted me with, "Remember that time you got a pussy willow stuck up your nose?" We had not spoken of it for forty-five years.

Life Lessons
- Even soft, small things in the wrong place can cause big problems.
- Silence can be painful.

MOM TO A GROWN-UP ME

In the later years of my mother's life, some of the best times she and I shared took place sitting around her kitchen table, chatting in the quiet before dawn.

We discussed current events, politics, and sports, but more often family and religion. My mother was a woman of unrelenting faith. She was a student of theology, scripture, and people. One morning, we wondered aloud how some religious leaders could proclaim beliefs with certainty that God was speaking directly through them. Our thoughts turned to churches and denominational debates on the theological implications of same-sex marriage, which led to my mentioning that I'd heard a member of our extended family had just announced that she was gay.

As I rose from the table to get another cup of coffee, Mom said, "Well, I don't think God cares what happens in bed between two consenting adults."

That's not what you thought when I was a teenager was all that I could think to say—but I didn't say anything.

Then I asked, "Do you think it's going to snow?" which was Mom's favorite way to change the subject.

Life Lessons

- Parents tell their kids things they need to hear when they are ready to want to hear them.
- Some things are never easy to talk about with your mother.

THE GREAT WALLS OF CHINA

My trip to China in 1996 occurred due to my great fortune of serving on the board of trustees of Appalachian State University, working to establish a "sister university" relationship with Fudan University in Shanghai. At the invitation of Fudan, Appalachian State sent a contingent of university leaders, teachers, and students to assess the receptivity of both educational institutions to form a mutually beneficial relationship. Since the current Appalachian board chair could not make the trip, I was most grateful to stand in for him as immediate past board chair.

Our first stop was Hong Kong, where I performed the most athletic feat of my life. Our group was hustling into a mall to do some last-minute shopping. Unlike American locations of commerce, this one had a four-inch stone threshold that tripped my right foot, sending my left foot to land and slide on polished marble until my leg extended completely. For the first time in my life, I did a full split. Behind me, I heard the same tripping sounds and, knowing that the sixty-five-year-old female college dean was right behind me, I torqued my torso, extended my arms, caught her face in one hand and her chest in the other, and lowered her to the stone surface.

After basking in praise and thanks for averting her injury, I had trouble getting off the floor. A few hours later, the burning and aching of my right upper leg made me wince with each step onto our flight to Shanghai. My traveling companions' group consensus: I had pulled my right groin.

◆　◆　◆

Throughout the next week, I limped and shuffled to our classes at Fudan and on the industrial tours that the business school arranged. My colleagues plied me with assorted painkillers. For some reason, I turned down our Chinese hosts' offers to arrange the healing art of acupuncture for me—a major mistake.

On Friday, we flew to Beijing for a weekend of sightseeing. We rose early on Saturday and walked miles through Tiananmen Square and the Forbidden City before heading to the Great Wall of China. Groin injury notwithstanding, I was not about to miss that world wonder. I didn't appreciate the steepness of the mountainous ridgeline upon which the wall stood, nor the hundreds of tall steps that I could climb only with my left leg, dragging my right behind me. That night, I skipped the group dinner in favor of a long hot bath, but the throbbing stabs of pain grew intense. Having exhausted my group's entire stash of painkillers, I finally headed for the hotel lobby shop, searching for pharmaceutical relief.

Inside the shop, a short, middle-aged woman in a blue embroidered dress greeted me with a bow and a smile. When I asked her if she had something for pain, she said,

"Yes! Yes!" But she didn't move, other than more bows and smiles. I asked her for aspirin, acetaminophen, ibuprofen, and every brand-name analgesic I could think of. More smiles and bows. Even "morphine" didn't register with her.

My desperation soaring, I decided to act out my pain. I feared that pointing to my groin might spark an international incident, so I went for a severe headache. I grimaced, put my open hands inches from each temple, gritted my teeth, shook my head from side to side, and moaned, "Oh! Ooooo! Hurt! Hurt!" and looked as pathetic as I could.

The woman's eyes widened. "Ah! Ah!" she said, her face beaming. She raised her index finger and began crooking it as if I should follow. She led me to a glass case, where she smiled, bowed, and pointed to the contents therein.

There were only two products in the entire case: a bottle of Phillips' Milk of Magnesia and a pack of Trojan condoms.

I bought a fifth of scotch.

Life Lessons
- When traveling abroad, learn some important keywords in advance.
- Being lost in translation can extend beyond mere words.

CHARLIE'S RADIATOR SHOP

Somewhere in the Arizona desert, just shy of the Grand Canyon, Dad announced, "We're about to flip 100,000!" His excitement was palpable, and he made my sisters and me look over his shoulder and watch the odometer of our 1955 Oldsmobile click to all zeros.

Three days later, on the last desert section of Route 66 heading west, our vintage radiator boiled over.

Inquiries in the closest small town led us to what looked like an open-air blacksmith's shed in an old Western—dirt floor, weathered tree trunks propping up a rusting tin roof that shaded a collection of twisted metal around a pit of fire boiling a bathtub of metal and rising steam. Brimstone came to mind.

Charlie was a huge man in bib overalls, no shirt, lips suspending a perpetually burning cigarette, the ashes of which collected in the burly patch of his chest hair. His glistening biceps were the size of ham hocks and his catcher's mitts for hands looked like they could crush a skull with a slight pinch. I backed away from him as he pounded the hot metal in his tongs into submission, his grin notwithstanding. But, in time, we learned that his formidable and frightening appearance belied the outpouring of empathy from this giant of a man when he learned that we should have been on our maiden voyage to Disneyland rather than his shop.

As it turns out, Disneyland was Charlie's favorite place on earth. Before we knew it, Charlie had called a taxi driver friend to take us to a "movie house" fifteen miles away where Walt Disney's *The Littlest Outlaw* was playing, so we could wait while he fixed our car in the theater's air-conditioned comfort (a luxury that Dad never felt necessary in his cars until 1970).

Two showings later, the taxi driver took us back to Charlie's, where my sisters and I watched him put his last touches on our radiator, mesmerized by his expert descriptions and advice about Disneyland. He told us which rides to skip, which not to miss, and in what order to maximize our time, value, and happiness. He tutored us about Disneyland's complex ABCDE ticket system. Charlie's favorite ride was the Mine Train, especially the underground section where a stream of clear, cool water flowed amid sparkling gems of every color.

Thanks to Charlie, when we walked down Main Street in Disneyland for the first time, we didn't feel like rookies.

Life Lessons
- Kindness can come in all types of packages.
- Wisdom from an experienced guide can be a precious gift.

CHALK TALK

In the fall of my junior year of high school, I was on a varsity football team that pundits predicted would repeat their annual claim to the title of New River District champions. Several All-District players returned, and an undefeated junior varsity team was ascending. The stars were aligned for our continued gridiron glory until one fell. The head coach who had led the team for years took a promotion in the school system. But not to worry; he recommended the team's longtime scout, who we knew was smart (he taught algebra, geometry, trigonometry, and probability), knew football, and was excited to be our new, first-time-ever head coach.

Fall came; leaves fell, as did our team's rankings.

We hadn't won all season, and our next game was on our home field against a cross-county rival that we usually beat. Yet at halftime, when my team and I moped into our locker room to hear what our coach would say, we were losing. We sat down on wooden benches that made a U around the blackboard, still chalked with optimistic pregame Xs and Os. We hung our heads and waited.

Only sighs of disgust and under-our-breath laments cut the sullen silence.

Suddenly, the blackboard exploded.

I looked up and saw heads ducking ricochets of white sticks of chalk. The remnants of a box lay on the floor under a cloud of chalk dust lingering in the air. We turned to see who had thrown a box of chalk with such power, and there our head coach stood, his face as red as a candy apple. We stared at him as he shouted, "You ain't nothing but a bunch of hermaphrodites! I wouldn't piss on you if your guts were on fire in the desert!"

We should have been horrified by his crass and thoughtless language. We should have been embarrassed that we'd set him into such a rage. But if he meant to rile us up and make us mad, his plan failed. We said nothing.

We had no idea what he meant.

In the hush that returned, I watched several teammates turn to each other and shrug as if to say, "Hell if I know." Then I heard someone whisper, "What's a hermaphrodite?"

We lost that night and went on to have a losing season.

◆ ◆ ◆

Postscript: That head coach coached many of us in that room to a winning record the next season—and he never berated us in such a way again. Perhaps he learned his lesson.

Life Lessons
- When giving a motivational talk, use words your audience can understand.
- If you give up on your team, they might give up on you.

THE GIFT OF A PACIFIER

One night before Christmas, our oldest son, Seth, despite parental cajoling and admonishments, was still attached to his pacifier, to which he would lovingly coo "My paci!" several times a day. A caring cousin had shared her success in suggesting to her child that he sacrifice his pacifier to the Easter Bunny, who would then give it to a little boy or girl somewhere who needed it more. Though we had our doubts, we explained to Seth that Santa Claus needed his pacifier for a needy child.

To our amazement, he pulled his own plug and placed his beloved "paci" on the plate of Santa's sugar cookies and Rudolph's raw carrots. Not one whimper, not one tear shed.

Throughout the next year, we shared our cousin's wisdom with our friends and enjoyed their accolades about our brilliant and creative parenting. Some suggested being honored as "Parents of the Year." If they only knew what awaited us.

Move with me now to the next Christmas Eve, when we found Seth alone in the living room, staring into the boughs of our decorated Fraser fir. Tears streaked his cheeks in prismatic streams.

"Oh, Seth. What in the world is the matter?" we asked.

He looked up, like a three-year-old Stoic in red flannel footie pajamas, and said, "I'm just wondering what thing I love Santa will take from me this year."

Life Lessons

- The message sent isn't always the message received.
- Adult logic wanders unknown paths in the heart of a child.

FAINTING IN THE HOLLAND TUNNEL

During the summer of 1964, before my eighth-grade year, our family's summer camping trip to New England and Canada was unique. For the first and only time, we took someone else with us. My first cousin Walt had been living in our basement while he attended Virginia Tech, and he remains the only person outside our immediate family foolish enough to climb into our Oldsmobile sedan with two other adults, two teenagers, and an eleven-year-old. Tight quarters they were, especially without air-conditioning or a cooler of ice, which Dad would explain away with "That's what windows are for" and "Ice just melts."

◆ ◆ ◆

On our route north, Dad decided that we should drive through New York City, perhaps hoping we'd absorb a smidgen of culture via some magical drive-by osmosis. From the New Jersey Turnpike, we turned toward the Holland Tunnel with Mom at the wheel, Dad riding shotgun and my little sister, Sarah Jane, between them. Cousin Walt sat behind Mom with Carol and me next to him. The rush hour traffic was bumper to bumper, moving at a good clip.

When the entrance to the tunnel came into sight, Mom began to emit a few of her *pshews*, a sign that our family well knew meant she was in distress.

"What is it, Sarah?" Dad asked.

"You know I can get claustrophobic in a tunnel."

"Just don't think about it," Dad said, "and you'll make it just fine."

Mom followed an eighteen-wheel tractor-trailer down into the smudgy darkness below the Hudson River. Another eighteen-wheeler came alongside us, and still another tractor-trailer closed in and rode our rear bumper. With our windows down, the noise was deafening and the exhaust fumes nauseating.

It was then that Mom said, "Dick, I'm going to faint!"

"No, you're not!" Dad insisted.

Walt lunged forward, extending his arms over Mom's shoulders, and grabbed the steering wheel with both hands. Dad commandeered the pedals with the toes of his size-twelve wingtips. Mom's head bowed forward, and while her hands fell away from the steering wheel, she never fainted.

And that's how we drove out of the end of that tunnel into the bright sunlight of New York City.

Life Lessons
- When one of your teammates drops the ball, pick it up and run with it.
- Always believe someone when they tell you that they are claustrophobic.

MY FIRST AND ONLY SNEAK-OUT

"Hello," I said into the telephone receiver.

"Richard. Craig. Can you spend the night tonight?"

My thirteen-year-old social calendar was as empty as usual. "Sure," I said, wondering why the last-minute invite.

"Great," Craig said. "Ginger and Brenda want us to sneak out with them tonight."

Am I dreaming? Did Christmas come two weeks early? Sneaking out was for cool Blacksburg upperclassmen. I had never snuck out once, much less with either of those two heartthrobs of our class, one of whom had started calling me "boyfriend" for reasons I could not fathom but cherished nonetheless. I took this invitation as a command performance, a test I must pass.

"I'm in," I said.

The girls connived a midnight rendezvous in a new house under construction in Brenda's neighborhood. Craig and I would have a thirty-minute walk to paradise. Easy peasy.

◆ ◆ ◆

After slipping out of Craig's house undetected, we began our trek through lawns and fields, avoiding streetlights and possible police encounters. We traveled under a clear moonlit sky among shadows of dark violet. Armed with the knowledge of our town's geography, we schemed our best path to the promised land. Or so we thought.

Our runaway imaginations had blinded us from reading a thermometer, the mercury of which hovered in the teens and was on its way to a single-digit low. We set a fast pace, trying to raise our body heat. When we came to a pasture neither of us remembered, we decided to take a shortcut through it, parting the barbed wire fence for each other like infantrymen on a mission.

Fifty yards in, a deep, guttural moan stopped us in our tracks.

"What was that?"

Then we heard thuds as if a sledgehammer was pounding the earth. Vicious snorts followed. There was something in this field. Then a black mass started to move in our direction. A thunderous bellow identified our monster, making us scream, "Bull! Run!"

We took off and sprinted until the ground under our feet vanished into a deep gully. Head over heels we tumbled, not stopping until we landed in a half-frozen creek. The bull stopped at the cliff's edge, snorted, pawed, and bellowed some more as we scampered up the other side. We bolted as fast as we could and flew over the next fence. On the other side, the high fives we exchanged sent needles down my forearms.

"We're alive!" Craig yelled as we marched onward.

Within minutes, our muddy shoes, pants, and coats glittered with ice crystals.

◆ ◆ ◆

We found the girls waiting for us at the rendezvous point. They led us to an open-air structure of wood framing around a gravel floor, upon which we sat and began what we were there to do. Neither Craig nor I mentioned the bull or why we were covered in ice. Neither of the girls asked.

After a few minutes of learning that kissing with chattering teeth risked chipping teeth, the girls thought of something else they'd rather do and bade us adieu.

On the way back to Craig's house, we walked under every streetlight and even right down the middle of Main Street, hoping a Good Samaritan or even a town cop would pity us and drive us home before we froze to death. No one came to our rescue.

My girlfriend dumped me the following week.

Life Lessons

· Icy hearts can fracture easily.
· Sneaking out can be hazardous to your health.

"FORKED"

As a member of the administrative staff of Presbyterian Hospital, I went to the medical staff lounge early one morning, where I encountered one of our esteemed surgeons stewing and mumbling in a state of heightened perturbance. This urologist took pride in calling himself a "West by God Virginian" who took no guff from anyone. Bracing myself for another assault on a possible mishap in some hospital area for which my team was responsible, I asked him what was wrong.

After spewing a string of expletives about the ancestry of his offenders, he blurted, "Last night, I got trenched!"

Lately, Charlotte teens had been driving their vehicles through lawns, leaving deep tire ruts or "trenches." The surgeon continued, "Tonight I'm going to hunker down in my front shrubs with my twelve-gauge and wait for them!" I could see him there, huddled behind a blind of azaleas in camouflage like Bill Murray in *Caddyshack*, and I couldn't help but chuckle.

"What are you laughing at? What if it happened to you?"

"I understand," I said. "Just this morning, I woke up to see a thousand white plastic forks impaling my front lawn. We'd been 'forked.'"

"Forks?"

"As in, 'Fork you.' And in the past two weeks, we've been egged and TP-ed too."

"God damn! Don't that make you want to kill those sons of bitches?"

"Not really."

"Why the hell not?"

Harking back to my teenage years, I said, "I deserve everything I get."

Life Lessons
- What goes around comes around.
- It is often wiser to laugh and clean up a mess than make a bigger one.

ROY ROGERS AND ME

A version of this story originally appeared in the Charlotte Observer *on 7/30/98.*

It's one of my earliest memories—twelve green bottle caps were strewn upon my bedspread. "Will these things really get me a Roy Rogers T-shirt?" I asked as my mother counted them aloud. I had never "saved up" for anything in my life. I was four years old.

Mom drove me somewhere—to a building with a parking lot is all I remember. When she came out, she carried the precious white garment emblazoned with a picture of rearing Trigger under the Double R Ranch sign. Roy Rogers was astride his regal palomino, waving his hat and smiling at me. Could life get any better?

I wore my Roy Rogers T-shirt every day Mom let me. I wore it while I watched his Saturday morning television show. I was Roy's helper. He had Trigger; I had my tricycle. Together we saved the girls in the neighborhood from the bad guys.

Roy helped me move from Lincolnton, North Carolina, to Blacksburg, Virginia, the next year. I wore my T-shirt everywhere to let the kids know I was one of the good guys.

Two years later, I wore my Roy Rogers T-shirt when I tried to jump a ditch at a house under construction across the street. I missed, and Roy and I fell between the earth and the tar-covered cinder blocks. As the rain of dirt filled my eyes, I tried to stay calm. *He would never cry*, I said to myself. I began hauling myself up and limped to my back door. When I opened the door, I saw I was late for supper. My mother's wide eyes told me that I looked worse than I felt.

◆ ◆ ◆

That was the last time I wore that shirt. Smudges of tar made Trigger legless and striped Roy like a tiger. I mourned the passing of my T-shirt to the basement rag can for paintbrush cleanup. Roy helped Dad too, I supposed, at the time.

Dad and I used to argue about Roy Rogers versus Tom Mix. Dad was a Mix man. He said Tom Mix was a real cowboy, unlike the singing kind, which I never understood because Dad listened to opera. None of the other fathers did. But Dad was a preacher, and they were different.

Once Dad showed me a picture of Tom Mix. I was shocked. How could my father admire a man who wore black from head to toe? Roy Rogers wore a white hat. His double six-guns were a gleaming silver, not flat black. The piping on Roy's Western shirts was smart and distinctive. Roy was the man.

Years later, when I became a dad to three sons, I regretted that they would not get to know Roy Rogers as I had. But I took them to see Luke Skywalker, and they got to know him. We've watched Luke wear white together. How much difference is there, really, between Roy's blazing six-guns, never drawn except to do justice, and Luke's lightsaber? How much difference is there between "happy trails to you" and "may the force be with you"?

As you ponder that question, "I'll keep smiling until then . . ."

Life Lessons
- Different times call for new heroes.
- Justice, faithfulness, friendship, and commitment can transcend time.

POWER OUTAGE

I was fortunate to participate in a naval scholarship program that commissioned me as an ensign in the Navy Medical Service Corps and was assigned to the Duke University NROTC unit to complete my graduate degree in health administration. Upon graduation, I became a newly minted lieutenant (junior grade), and after three weeks of orientation school at Bethesda Naval Hospital, I was ordered to the administrative staff of Portsmouth Naval Hospital, a tertiary medical center that served the Norfolk area. In addition to my regular duties, I was an administrative watch officer, a night/weekend administrator, once every six weeks. Janice couldn't believe that a twenty-five-year-old with no hospital experience would be responsible for a one-thousand-bed teaching hospital for any length of time. I had to admit she had a point.

One evening early in my administrative watch officer tenure, after making rounds and finding things quiet, I retired to the watch sleeping quarters to catch a few winks. The phone woke me up.

The night chief, the noncommissioned officer who stayed up all night at the watch desk, said, "Lieutenant Howerton, the power is out."

My first thought was, *Why is he calling me?* All hospitals have emergency power generators for essential equipment, egress lighting, and at least one elevator. I said something like, "OK. Emergency generators."

"That's the problem. The emergency generators aren't working. We have no power. None."

"Are you kidding me?" (Not the most professional military response in a crisis.)

"No, sir. Engineering is working on it. Power company knows."

Up and in uniform, I ran into the hallway and looked out the window toward the main hospital tower. The sight stopped me in my tracks. Across the courtyard, a sixteen-story monolith of white bricks and black windows rose in the moonlight. My mind screamed, "Good God! I'm in charge of this?"

I bolted to the watch desk and found the night chief on the phone making notes. When he saw me, he put a hand over the mouthpiece and reported six patients were being Ambu-bagged by hand in the ICU, the OR had an emergency case proceeding by flashlight, the staff was reacting well overall, and engineering was working on the problem in the control room. Then he returned to his call.

I took off for the control room, a central location for monitoring and controlling all major systems. There, the night plant engineer explained that when the neighborhood power went off, the emergency generator switch engaged, but it had "over-revved" somehow and shut itself down. He'd tried to restart the generators three times with no success.

"Can it be fixed?"

"Yes. But it won't be a short fix."

I knew if I didn't do something to fix this, many people could get hurt. Lives could be on the line. *Do something!*

I ran back to the chief and told him I wanted to talk to the power company. As he dialed the number, the chief reminded me he'd already called them, and then he handed me the receiver.

I asked for my watch officer counterpart at the power company and told him who I was and that we had no power.

The power company night manager said, "So I've been told."

"We need power now!" The frantic tone of my voice sounded pitiful.

After a slight pause, the manager said, "Your emergency generators should get you—"

"But that's the problem! The emergency generators failed. We have no power at all. Nothing."

I was prepared to tell him about the six Ambu bags, the case in the OR by flashlight, and sixteen floors with no elevator. I was prepared to beg. But as it turns out, I didn't have to.

"That's different," came the suddenly brisk voice on the other line. "Here's what we'll do. You are now our number one priority. We will take down neighborhoods and reroute power to you as soon as possible." His voice was calm, controlled, and professional—the kind I wished mine had sounded like when I called. "It shouldn't take long," he said before hanging up.

The power came back on in less than fifteen minutes. Thanks to the amazing work of our night staff and the swift action of the night manager on duty at the power company, there were no adverse patient events.

Life Lessons

- In an emergency, clear and calm communication is crucial.
- "Night watch" professionals can be critical to saving lives.

WHEN TO WORRY

One hot afternoon during our torturous two-a-day August football practices, Assistant Coach Bill Brown had me hitting the seven-man blocking sled. This contraption was not one of the sleek metal gliders a coach could ride like a Roman charioteer. Rather, our obstruction was an antique contraption of railroad ties, assembled at angles with huge rusty nuts and bolts. The opponent my shoulder was "attacking" was a swath of weathered olive canvas stitched over leaking sawdust to a slab of timber in front of a huge spring that last flexed its rust-free self during the Great Depression. Our sled hadn't moved in years; dandelions and ragweed grew among its timbers. It could stop a tank.

My drill was solitary, my effort pathetic. Instead of a forceful *wham* that the first-string linemen delivered, my shoulder's paltry blows sounded more like a *poof*. My grandmother could have done better.

"Again," Coach Brown said to me.

Poof.

Again," he said one, two, six more times.

As I hit the sled again and again, I was certain that I would never make it through that day. *What kind of stupid idiot plays this game! I should just walk off and quit!*

I prayed that Coach Brown would move on to another fool who was more worthy of his attention.

But he didn't. Instead, he called me by name. "Richard, when I give up on you is when you need to worry. Try again."

I hit the sled with everything I had left within my diminished self.

"Good. Next!"

From that day forward until my final Friday night game, Coach Brown kept trying to make me a better player. For that I am forever grateful.

Life Lessons
- Don't take correction as criticism.
- A good coach or boss teaches skills; a great coach or boss teaches important life lessons.

BRITISH SCHOOLBOYS

My father's dream of taking his family camping in Europe began in June of 1965 in the small principality of Luxembourg, not because it was a central starting point for such a journey, but because that's where Icelandic Airlines' cheapest flights landed.

On our first nights in our tent, rain and mist christened us for seventy-two hours. All this precipitation did not concern us because five swaths of flat earth stair-stepped up the hill, upon which tents could be pitched on level planes. We took a spot on the lowest terrace.

Despite the weather, everything was working well. But then, a water main broke on the uppermost terrace. From our campsite below, we could see an ugly mass of mud creeping down the hillside from one terrace to the next, not unlike *The Blob* in the old horror movie—it was dark and hungry, devouring everything in its path. And it was headed right for us.

We panicked. After only three nights in Europe, this oozing muddy mass was about to engulf our home and all our possessions. There was no time to move or take down the tent. In a frenzy, our family started digging a divertive trench around our tent. But our attempts were pathetic, gouging with one claw hammer, our fingers, and our heels.

At the peak of our desperation, we heard a distinct British-accented voice say, "Say, Yanks. Could use some help there?" A man in a Smokey Bear hat and khaki uniform stood in front of a company of schoolboys, all shouldering collapsible shovels like those infantrymen use to dig foxholes. I had seen this group down the way, kicking soccer balls in ways that seemed impossible.

"Yes!" Dad yelled.

The troop flew into action, digging and scraping a series of interlocking trenches, moats, dams, and even a plank bridge that would have been the envy of World War I generals. When the mud wall hit our terrace, the schoolboys' earthworks channeled the mud around our tent fortress. We were saved.

We tried to thank the Brits for their help. But they made light of their task and declared our praise and thanksgiving superfluous. As the schoolmaster led his lieges away, he said, "Think nothing of it, Yanks. World War II and all, you know."

Life Lessons
- Don't go camping without a shovel.
- Allies remember. Pay it forward.

LOST IN TRANSLATION

On the last night of my two-week trip to Fudan University with faculty and students from Appalachian State in 1996, we had a celebratory dinner on the Huangpu River across from the glittering lights of the futuristic Pudong District of Shanghai. We enjoyed the last meal that we would share with our delightful university host and guide, a young nuclear physicist. Around our table sat the ASU chancellor, the provost, two deans, a history professor, and I, taking turns to thank this impressive woman who had shepherded us every day of our visit.

To my left, our professor struggled to get slippery noodles out of the serving bowl and onto his plate. After several attempts, he added vocal encouragement to his task, emitting a plaintive, "Come on, baby."

Our Chinese guide leaned in and asked, "What means, 'Come on, baby'?"

We smiled and took turns explaining that it was an idiom, a colloquial expression of encouragement, in this case to help with the process of serving his plate, probably talking to himself as much as to the noodles.

Our host smiled and nodded as if it all made perfect sense to her.

After desserts, we asked her if there was anything we could do for her to convey our gratitude beyond our effusive thanks for her wonderful helpfulness.

"Yes," she said. "I need to understand better young Americans' expressions like 'Come on, baby.'"

We jumped in like eager schoolkids educating our teacher for a change. We chipped in several current colloquialisms, providing explanations of connotations of things not literally said. My contribution to her was "chill out." Our host seemed to understand our interpretations, and we basked in the glow of our success and her appreciation.

Then she said, "My last group of college students said something that I didn't understand. I wish you could explain it to me."

"Of course! What was it?" we sang in unison.

"What means 'ass-kisser'?"

We couldn't help but laugh as we offered one explanation, then another. But for the next ten minutes, despite our best attempts, we discovered that none of us highly educated and experienced professional communicators could explain what "ass-kisser" meant to our young female nuclear physicist host. Pointing out that "brown-noser" meant something similar elicited a blanker stare. No interpretation, literal or figurative, registered with her. Slowly, our loquaciousness gave way to our silent acceptance that we could not give her what she had asked of us.

After hugs, our host left us for the night. We sat and discussed our failure to communicate such a simple concept. We began to appreciate that in China, it was a given that people in positions of authority were to be honored and respected, so much so that it was impossible to convey that a subordinate should not kowtow or "suck up" to a superior. In our culture, kissing ass and brown-nosing were pejorative acts worth condescension; in her culture, such respectful behavior was expected, and to hold someone doing so in contempt was inconceivable to her.

Our trip to China ended with an admission that some bridges between cultures can only be crossed with great difficulty, if at all.

Life Lessons

· Sometimes, we cannot give what someone asks of us despite our best intentions.

· Sometimes, there are simply no words.

WAKING UP NEXT TO A BRAND-NEW SOMETHING

When we entered the western gate of Glacier National Park in July of 1962, our mountain high began with a frolic in snow left from winter and Dad spying something he'd never seen before: a Rocky Mountain goat jumping from one ledge to another, hundreds of feet above us. We drove down into the valley as the setting sun cast a golden-peachy glow over maroon mountains and into a brand-new camping ground, another first for us. It was so new, unfinished perhaps, that the workers had left a flatbed trailer with a huge, corrugated metal drainage pipe equipped with some sort of contraption with a fenced opening right next to our tent site.

After pitching our tent and grabbing a bite, we went to the park ranger's slide presentation on the flora and fauna of the park. With the universe winking starlight across the black sky, my father beamed with satisfaction of having had a perfect day of family camping and a shared wonder of God's creation.

Dad carried his euphoria into the following morning as we broke camp to continue our journey eastward. I accompanied him to the park ranger's office to check out. Dad thanked the ranger again for his inspiring slideshow and the brand-spanking-new campground.

"Thank you, sir," the ranger said. "You are some of the first ones to use our newest campground. In fact, it's so new that the grizzlies haven't wanted to give up their previous stomping grounds."

"Grizzly bears?" Dad asked.

"Yes, sir. Did you see the bear trap we parked down there?" the ranger asked.

As he described it, my father's face changed color from the healthy pink of proud fatherhood to the bleached white of a pulpit dress shirt.

We had slept the previous night right next to a grizzly bear trap.

Life Lessons

- First impressions are not always what they seem.
- Learn what a bear trap looks like before you go camping.

WEIGH BOY: PART I

In 1972, before my senior year in college, summer jobs in Blacksburg were scarce. So, when Mom decided to purchase pavement for our gravel driveway, she negotiated a job for me from its source—the asphalt plant and quarry owned by Adams Construction Company on the outskirts of town.

The asphalt plant stood perched on top of a hill that had been bulldozed to create a flat expanse of crushed limestone above the working quarry hundreds of feet below. A single rail fence marked the edge of the quarry cliff. Midway down the hill toward the quarry entrance sat the crushers, machines that munched boulders into gravel and sorted them by size. The smallest stones went to the asphalt plant, a humongous gray contraption of tanks, hoses, and conveyor belts atop a steel trestle. When fully operational, the plant spits out steaming black magma into the beds of dump trucks waiting beneath it.

During a loading run, my job was to watch the stone conveyor and pick out random sticks, leaves, trash, or too-large rocks that would spoil the batch being blended inside the elevated tanks. I worked hard and kept my head down, especially since my new employer gave hiring priority to returning Vietnam veterans. My college deferment did nothing to endear me to my coworkers, who had slogged through rice paddies, survived firefights, and exchanged tales of atrocities committed by combatants both seen and unseen.

After fumbling around for a couple of weeks, I was offered a promotion to man the scales that weighed trucks. I jumped at the chance to work in the clapboard shack weigh station, even with its closed doors and windows to keep the dust off the electric scale mechanism, because it came with air-conditioning. I was tired of going home caked in limestone dust sticking to my sweat and smelling like tar. My coworkers sneered at my new privilege and changed my name from "College Boy" to "Weigh Boy."

True to my new title, I weighed trucks that drove onto the platform outside my window by sliding weights until everything balanced on a machine that looked like an old doctor's scale for giants. When the glass-covered dial stopped moving, I inserted a card and the machine stamped out its findings in red ink. Two stamps per truck, first empty, then full; the difference was the net weight that determined the value of the load, either asphalt or stone.

One morning, the hill boss came into the weigh station and announced that he was down a couple of drivers. He asked me if I could drive a stick. I'd driven four-on-the-floor cars for years, so I answered yes. The next thing I knew, he took my weigh stool, and I was at the wheel of an old reject dump truck with air brakes and ten gears—five forward, each with a high and low. I was to make runs from the piles of quarried stone on the top of the hill down to the crushers. Somehow, I managed to get that old beat-up, stripped-down, seatbelt-and-mirror-less, for-quarry-use-only beast to the rock heaps. There, a front loader dumped load after load into my truck bed, each one lowering my view of the horizon. Then the front loader driver waved me off.

Loaded with more than twenty thousand pounds of stone, my old truck was harder to get moving. I had to shift gears several times to get it over to the slope that led down to the crushers. Once I turned downhill, my speed increased rapidly. Too rapidly. *You should have kept it a lower gear*, I shouted to myself, pressing the brakes to slow down. But my descent accelerated. I stomped the brake pedal to the floor. Then pumped it. Nothing happened but more speed.

Sweat began coursing down my spine. *Do something!* my brain screamed. *Downshift!* I tried, but the sound of grinding metal told me I couldn't downshift. *Change course! Quarry cliff on your right! Trees and a gully on your left; a dead stop! Ram this runaway into a pile of stone! Or traverse the hill!*

I yanked the wheel toward the oaks but kept pulling it until I was headed back up the hill. My lungs let me breathe as the truck slowed to a stop. And then, the truck started rolling backward down the hill. *You idiot! You're in neutral! With no brakes! Jump out!* Blind to what I was rolling toward and picking up speed, I steered in what I hoped was the direction of the crusher piles and reached for the door handle.

Suddenly, my head whiplashed into the metal behind me as my rig slammed to a halt. When my vision cleared, I switched off the ignition and slid out, rubbing the knot rising on the side of my head. A crowd gathered around my truck, protruding out of a mound of gravel. Among the chortles and guffaws, I heard, "Weigh Boy can't even drive a truck!" and other more colorful descriptions of my driving skill.

My boss ran down from the weigh station and got my story. I told him that he could fire me on the spot, but I was never driving a dump truck again. Then I staggered up the hill to reclaim my stool.

◆ ◆ ◆

Later that afternoon, my boss came to see me. We were alone when he told me, "There was a reason your air brakes didn't work. There was a break in the line. They wouldn't hold pressure. You were lucky you hit that pile."

I don't remember saying anything. The boss headed toward the door, stopped, and turned back toward me.

"That air hose break—it was more like a cut," he said. "Hard to say, but it could've been a fresh one. We'll never know." Then he left.

There is no doubt in my mind that that air hose was cut. By whom, the hill boss could not or would not find out. Since no one was badly hurt, live and let live, right? From that day on, the hardcore Vietnam vets never harassed me again. It was as if I had passed some sort of test or trial.

Not another word was ever said to me about what happened that day on the quarry hill.

Life Lessons
- Don't drive something you don't know how to control.
- Don't work where you're not wanted.

TUMMY TICKLE

When I became a father, I intended to give my boys at least one of the "out West" trips my parents had given me. Janice was on board with my plan to cram our Toyota van with the two of us plus our fifteen-, thirteen-, and four-year-old sons and drive six thousand miles in eighteen days. But she let it be known that she had four hundred dollars in cash stashed away for a one-way flight back to Charlotte at any time, should her husband and boys' combined testosterone reach a toxic level.

On our second night, we checked into the Chicago Marriott for a last metropolitan exposure before heading across the plains. After schlepping our suitcases to our room on the twenty-fifth floor, we decided to head back down an afternoon walk on the Miracle Mile of Michigan Avenue. When the elevator doors opened, we were greeted by the warm smile of a young bellman in proper hotel regalia. He held the door for us with the grace and confidence of a well-trained professional.

As luck would have it, the elevator began a nonstop drop toward the lobby. While four-year-old Rob had ridden elevators before, he had never felt the light-headed effects of a rapid high-rise descent. "Ooooo!" he said. "That makes my tummy tickle!"

Janice and I exchanged isn't-he-cute grins with the pleasant young bellman.

"Actually," Rob said. "It's not my tummy. It's my penis!" The only sounds in the cab were five gasps. Janice and I stared at Rob, hoping to keep him quiet. But he wasn't through.

"You know, Mom," Rob said, looking at Janice. "We haven't talked about my penis in a long time."

The bell rang on the lobby landing, and—notwithstanding his world-class customer service training—who can blame the young professional bellman for falling out of the cab, doubling over with forearms crossing his convulsing abdomen, and losing roaring guffaws that echoed within the three-story atrium?

We didn't hang around for a teaching moment, grateful that his histrionics provided cover for us to slink toward the Miracle Mile.

Life Lessons
- Kids speak from their heart, gut, and everywhere else.
- Sometimes, even the most professional training can be broken by a well-timed penis confession.

UNINVITED RIDERS

Despite being veterans of camping in the United States, European camping in the summer of 1965 presented several surprises and challenges. Back home, campgrounds numbered their tent sites like motel rooms, spaced them yards apart for privacy, and provided each a picnic table and, more often than not, a grilled fireplace to cook on. In contrast, European campers spread themselves out in a field, picking a spot that wasn't too close to a neighbor where they could unfold their tables, ignite portable propane burners, and plop themselves in chairs they'd brought to create a home away from home. It all seemed very civilized—until we got to London. There, in our campground that overlooked the original site of the long-demolished Crystal Palace, tents were pitched ten deep with only inches between them. Walking through this chaos of canvas was like running an obstacle course of ropes, stakes, tables, chairs, and all sizes and types of people scattered upon an expanse of grassless gravel.

One morning, we left our disarray of accommodations to tour the city. Before we headed off to see Big Ben and

Buckingham Palace, Dad parked our VW Microbus near the camp office and went in to get a map. It was a warm day, and we left the VW's doors open. Mom was in the front passenger seat reading, and for some reason, all three of us kids were in the back-back seat. After a few minutes, two strangers, college-aged guys, got into our VW and sat in the middle seat. Then they closed the door and began conversing in a foreign language.

This intrusion did not concern any of us. My Baptist preacher father never met a stranger. Back home, he surprised us often with spur-of-the-moment visitors and dinner guests. We figured Dad had met some foreign students and invited them to tag along. We kids returned to our horsing around and Mom to her London guidebook.

When Dad came back, he hopped in the driver's seat, started the car, and took off. Mom's navigation commands consumed his attention. The rest of us stayed quiet. About halfway into our journey, Dad noticed the strange faces in the rearview mirror and introduced himself. Fortunately, the two guys spoke English, and we learned that they were Dutch college students who had mistaken our Microbus for the campground's shuttle into town.

The Dutch dudes ended up being great guys. They knew London from previous visits and helped with logistics and sightseeing advice. My sisters were in heaven, having hit the good-looking-guys-trapped-in-our-car jackpot. The Dutch guys toured with us for most of the day, sharing their knowledge of many previous trips. When we departed, hugs and addresses were exchanged. My sisters remained giddy for weeks, and when they returned to Blacksburg, the ensuing foreign correspondence thrilled them all over again.

Life Lessons
- Be open to serendipitous events; they might lead to something good.
- Make sure the right people are on the bus.

TIME MANAGEMENT PRIORITY

As a young healthcare executive, I was always searching for clues to better manage my time. I read articles and attended seminars, where I sat at the feet of personal productivity experts, taking notes and adapting their techniques to combat my propensity to procrastinate and daydream.

The best solution that I found went something like this:

a. Make an unnumbered list of tasks you need to accomplish.

b. Assign "1" to the most important task.

c. Assign "2" to the next most important task.

d. Stop assigning numbers.

e. Work on accomplishing the number 1 task and nothing but the number 1 task until it is accomplished.

f. Then work on number 2 until it is done.

g. Assign a new 1 and 2.

h. Repeat.

It worked for a while. But when I tried to apply it to my life, there were games to be played with the definitions of *need* and *importance*. Wasn't it also important to achieve something quickly and feel a sense of accomplishment to propel ourselves onward? If so, why not assign 1 and 2 to things most easily completed? Or, in the name of workplace happiness, why not assign priorities to what we enjoy doing? Why not reward ourselves with happy work—didn't we fight for our independence for the pursuit of happiness? Or, since every task on the list is important and must be done anyway, why not just jump around as the mood suits us? And so it went.

◆ ◆ ◆

One day, a colleague and I commiserated about our daily workload over green plastic trays in the hospital cafeteria. I shared my dread about a task on my list that I was certain would make me miserable if I confronted it.

She looked at me and said, "I'm amazed that you've been so successful without knowing that what you dread most is absolutely the most important thing for you to do first." Her quiet confidence conveyed that she'd known that basic fact of life since kindergarten.

I chuckled.

"I'm serious," she said. "Think about it. You might find that the thing you dreaded wasn't even a big deal. Or you might find that it is, and then you can deal with it, fix it, and not have to worry about it anymore."

I tried it. She was right. It is the best time management advice that I have ever received.

Life Lessons
- The thing you dread most is probably the first thing you should deal with.
- Talking to a trusted colleague about what's troubling you can help in unpredictable ways.

A MOVING POUND CAKE

My mother's Sunday dinners always included a dessert that was photo-ready for the cover of *Better Home and Gardens*. The possible exception was her pound cake, which was outwardly deceptive, like a great novel with a torn plain cover. The ingredients of her ancestral recipe echoed its name: a pound of flour, a pound of sugar, a pound of eggs, and a pound of butter. When served, its concocted appearance was faulty—not in an error-prone sense, but rather of the San Andreas variety. When Mom extracted her masterpiece from her heirloom tube cake pan, cracks creased the cake crust that ringed the middle hole, exposing crevasses of butter-yellow hints of the deliciosity that lay beneath its honey-brown surface.

One Sunday, Mom delegated the baking of her pound cake to my sister and her best friend, as she had done a few times before to great success. Throughout our meal, delectable aromas of baking pound cake wafted around the dining room table. When it came time to present the final course, Mom served it on a cut glass pedestal, a regal presentation to behold as if her creation should reign over the plates and dessert forks in waiting. We oohed and aahed on cue.

Then, the cake moved.

That was new. Mom's cakes didn't move, but this one began to list like a ship with a gash below its waterline. The sight transfixed us. Just as Mom reached for it, the top of the cake slid down toward her white linen tablecloth on a lava flow of uncooked batter.

My sister and her friend ran to the kitchen and hurried back with the cake pan and spatulas to return the batter and underbaked bits to the oven.

We learned later that the cake bakers of the day, whether distracted by the cute male guests my father had invited to our table or by their mesmerizing dialogue about them, must have set the timer wrong. They also confessed that they'd tested the cake's doneness by inserting a tooth-pick into it and pulling it out to see if it was "clean" of batter versus the instrument the recipe called for—a long broomstick straw.

Less than an hour later, Mom served her first and last patchwork pound cake. It was delicious.

Life Lessons
- Things may appear fully baked when they really aren't.
- When you create a mess, scoop it up, fix it, and serve it again.

ARE YOU JAMES FORD?

About three weeks after I took a new job as CEO of Alamance County Hospital in Burlington, North Carolina, I was awakened in the middle of the night by Janice's elbow stabbing my ribs. Before I could protest, my sleep-filled eyes made out flashing blue lights traversing our bedroom ceiling. They could only mean one thing: *The police are here!*

Despite my exhaustion from dealing with the challenges of a dead-stopped construction project, a medical staff who had given the previous CEO a vote of no confidence, nurses threatening to strike, and trying to meet and make the best first impressions with as many doctors, board members, county commissioners, community leaders, citizens, neighbors, and hospital employees on all three shifts as I could, my mind fired awake with possibilities. These blue lights of the law brought yet another challenge to be mastered with confident forthrightness. I threw on my bathrobe, and by the time I made the short walk to the front door, I'd donned the capable-CEO-in-charge persona I'd been trying to sport for weeks.

Through the side windows flanking the front door, I saw two uniformed officers standing on the porch, gripping long flashlights, silhouetted by the headlights of their patrol car.

Steeled in executive posture, I opened the door, and in my strongest authoritative voice, I asked, "What can I do for you, officers?"

A beam of light hit my face. One of the officers asked, "Are you James Ford?"

I was not expecting that. Why would they ask that? Who is James Ford, and what could he have to do with a new emergency unfolding at the hospital that I would need to confront?

I must have stood there considering for some time, because Janice whispered behind me, "Say something."

Then it hit me. We were in a rental house, and we'd been receiving mail addressed to a presumed former tenant, James Ford. *That's it! I figured it out!*

I took a step forward and said, "No, officers. But I used to be."

The officers looked at each other and shrugged. One of them pushed his cap until its bill covered his eyes and raised his head to face his partner, saying, "Well, we got us another one."

Janice kicked me and said, "Say something else!"

I did. But it was too late. Despite introducing myself and explaining my response, the officers left and told some firefighters, who told the EMTs, who told the ER staff, who told the nurses. By the time I got to work the next day, a new nameplate had appeared on my desk that said James Ford. The whole hospital—which eventually included a red-faced me—laughed at my "executive" antics that day.

Life Lessons
- When someone asks you if you are someone else, just say no.
- You are never as in charge of a situation as you might think.

PARIS RIOT

Two nights after our muddy rescue by the British schoolboys in Luxembourg in June of 1965, my family was in
Paris, camping in the city's great park, the Bois de Boulogne.

After days of museum, cathedral, and tower tours, Mom
let it be known that she had dreamed her entire life of going to a real beauty parlor in Paris. It would be her private
splurge. I was surprised because Mom was used to "rough-
ing it" on our trips, and Dad's frugality made our travel
possible. But this was Paris, and Mom had her heart set
and her foot down on fulfilling her dream. So, on our last
afternoon in Paris, we deposited my mother at a Parisian
salon on a busy street somewhere between the Paris Opera
House and the President's Palace on the Champs-Élysées.

The rest of us tooled around lazily for a couple of hours
and then circled back to pick her up. Dad double-parked
our still-new VW Microbus on the other side of the street
since there were no parking spaces to be found. Mom wasn't
ready yet, and when Dad turned the key to begin circling
again, our VW wouldn't start. Dad went into a nearby shop
to use a phone, then returned and said a mechanic was on

the way. And there we sat as rush hour traffic thickened. Car horns and driver gestures told us that other drivers were not happy with us.

Suddenly, the traffic disappeared and an odd sense of vacancy descended upon us. Our position in the street gave us a clear view forward and aft. Ahead in the distance, an angry mob filled the street—and they were coming toward us. Young people were shouting and chanting as they marched, their fists raised in defiance. Out of our rear window, we saw mounted police, gendarmes armed with submachine guns, riding toward the mob and us. Both forces glared at the other. We were stuck in the middle of whatever was going to happen.

About that time, Mom emerged from the beauty parlor across the street. I'll never forget the way she looked. She stood in the only Sunday dress she'd brought for the trip, her hair and face fixed like a magazine model. Her smile and face were beaming with pride. It was the first time I realized my mother was a pretty woman.

Then she looked left and right, and her eyes widened and her face blanched. Just when I thought her panic might freeze her in place, my mother hiked up her skirt, ran across the wide boulevard, and hopped in with us, where we exchanged a few frantic exchanges like "Drive away!" "We can't!" and "We're going to die!"

But before my father could react, the mob in front of us halted their advance. They started milling around, still shouting and singing, and slowly dispersed. Minutes later, the police reined their horses around and went the other way.

Everything returned to normal, as did the obnoxious honks and hand gestures aimed our way. A few minutes later, the VW mechanic whom Dad had summoned by phone came riding up on his bicycle. He informed us that we had witnessed the annual University of Paris end-of-exams riot. He explained that the police were on hand only because Charles de Gaulle was hosting a state dinner at the palace and wanted to keep the students' vulgarity at a safe distance.

Life Lessons
- Even when you're dressed your best and expertly coiffed, it's good to be nimble on your feet.
- Too much studying can make you crazy.

WHEN YOU THINK YOU MIGHT HAVE A BRAIN TUMOR

For two weeks in my thirtieth year of life, I thought I might have a brain tumor.

It started one morning when three somber physicians came into my office and shut the door. They were not on my calendar. These doctors—my ENT, our hospital's neuroradiologist, and my internist, who was also the chief of the medical staff—broke the news that they wanted me to go to see a specialist at Duke because the X-rays I'd had recently for a sinus infection looked ominous. They would make the appointment for me as soon as possible. "We want to rule out the possibility that you might have a brain tumor," my physician said.

They said more, but I didn't hear much after "brain tumor."

The first available appointment was two weeks away. I spent the time waiting in private introspection, soul-searching, and fear. I told no one, not even Janice, because why worry her that she could become a widow with two sons under four if it turned out to be nothing? I began to make promises to God and myself. If I survived, I promised to try to be a better man. I promised to admit when I was wrong and say I'm sorry more quickly. I promised to apologize to those I thought I had wronged and ask for their forgiveness.

The specialist at Duke assured me right away that I had "nothing to worry about." He had compared my newest sinus X-rays with those taken four years earlier at Portsmouth Naval Hospital when I had a previous sinus infection. He concluded that I had a congenital mass of cartilage behind my left eye that looked suspicious, but it was unchanged and, therefore, harmless. "Nothing to worry about," he said again. I was out of his office in five minutes.

Life went on, but things were different. Some events seemed to slow so that I could appreciate happenings in the moment, while other things demanded I confront them with a new sense of urgency. In the confusing swirl and swerve between slow and urgent, I remembered my promises and tried to live up to them. Some colleagues noticed the change in me and shared that I didn't seem to be as much of the take-no-prisoners jerk that I once was.

In the next twelve months, I sought out two former best friends with whom I'd terminated contact due to silly circumstances to which I'd attached great significance. I had missed them and sought them out, eventually traveling several thousand miles to visit each of them. From others with whom I've shared this story, I am aware that asking for forgiveness for old transgressions can be resented if it uncovers feelings that they would rather have left buried. In my case, each of my childhood friends received me with surprise and welcome, and each listened to me apologize and share the past events that had led to my severing our relationship and weighed on my heart.

After listening to my saga of guilt and regret, each had the same reaction: "What are you talking about?" Neither had shared the pain I'd experienced. They didn't even remember the same specific events. They had moved on. They said they forgave me but seemed unsure it was necessary.

I am friends with both today. I only wish it hadn't taken me so many years to reach out.

Life Lessons

- A scare about one's mortality is an opportunity to reflect on what is truly important in life.
- Seek forgiveness, but accept that your apology may be more important to you than the person you believe you've harmed.

SICK IN REIMS

When my family arrived in Reims, France, our tent was still wet from rain the night before, so Dad decided to check the five of us into a single room in a pension—a hole-in-the-wall hotel with a floor of rooms perched over a street-level business. We ate dinner in the café next door, and the next morning, my stomach ached. Mom and Dad decided to leave me there, let me rest, and come back and get me after their visit to the city's famous cathedral.

A few minutes after they departed, a wave of nausea sent me scurrying to the bathroom down the hall, where my gastrointestinal tract erupted in both directions. Back in the room, abdominal cramps racked me as I thrashed among bedsheets between dashes to the sink to throw up. I moaned and groaned, hoping that someone might hear me and keep me from dying alone in my fourteenth year of life.

Someone did hear me. An old woman peered around the doorframe and asked me something I did not understand. I replied with another dash toward the sink, but I made it only as far as the odd not-a-sink-not-a-commode ceramic thing on the floor. The old woman uttered something and left me hugging what I learned later was called a bidet.

The old woman returned a few moments later and helped me get back in bed. After shuffling over with her stooped back to clean up my mess, she sat on the edge of my bed. She wore a white apron over a blue shift. Her white hair was knotted in a bun. She smiled at me and began whispering and cooing unknown words of comfort as she wiped my face with a cool, wet cloth. Then, she presented a tray holding two sugar cubes and a miniature glass of clear liquid. Her gray eyes looked at the tray and then at me. She nodded and smiled. She handed me a sugar cube. I ate it. Then, she put the shot glass in my hand and nodded. I shallowed its vile and bitter liquid in one gulp. Then she fed me another cube of sugar. She held my hand, stroking my hair and singing foreign lullabies until I fell asleep.

I was alone and groggy when my family returned. They loaded me into our Microbus, and I wasn't coherent enough to tell them my tale of woe and deliverance by the hands of my angel of mercy until much later that evening.

I never knew my angel's name. But I have never forgotten her acts of kindness, and I hope I never will.

Life Lessons
- Don't leave your children alone when they are sick—especially when they don't know the local language.
- A stranger's kindness can live forever.

A SECONDARY EMOTION

One day at work at the hospital, I found myself stewing over something or other that had gone wrong. I knew I was about to lose control in ways that did not "walk the talk" of our corporate values that I taught at employee orientation. I decided the best course of action was to hole myself up in my office and slam some drawers in solitude until I could figure out how to make things right.

I cleared my calendar, except for an appointment later that afternoon with a manager who reported to me. She was a thoughtful person, a master-degreed nurse, and an "old soul" as deemed by her Cherokee medicine man grandfather. Within the first minute of our meeting, she asked, "What is wrong?"

I must have told her what was troubling me that day because she returned with another question. "But why are you so angry?"

"I just told you," I snapped. "Weren't you listening?"

"You did tell me things, but not why you feel so angry," she said in a therapeutic voice that immediately infuriated me.

What is she talking about? I repeated the problem, layering in causations, circumstances, and potential reactions. She listened and asked, "You are still not telling me what or who hurt you."

"Hurt? What are you talking about?"

She took off her glasses, cleaned them, and put them on her head like a hairband. Then she looked at me and asked, "Richard, don't you know that anger is a secondary emotion to hurt? People don't get angry without being hurt first. Anger doesn't just happen. It's their reaction to hurt."

Her questions and proclamations stumped me, but her voice conveyed no doubt. I wondered if she had learned that piece of wisdom from graduate school or her grandfather. In either case, I took what she said as truth long enough to think back to what had happened before I got so mad. After a while, I understood what she meant, and as calm settled over me, I figured out what I needed to do next.

◆ ◆ ◆

Over the next several days, I wondered how I had managed to live thirty-seven years without knowing the wisdom that manager shared. Since then, her words have helped me examine and solve problems that I could have struggled with for much longer. And more times than I would like to admit, I've had to confront that I was angry with my own actions or inactions. Too often, I had done something wrong and was angry with myself, and if I weren't careful, I could take it out on others by making them think I was angry with them.

Life Lessons

- Anger is a byproduct of feeling hurt. If you are angry at someone, try to find and acknowledge the source of your hurt.
- Life-changing wisdom can come to you when you least expect it.

LOVE IN FLORENCE

Six weeks into our summer-long family camping trip
through Europe in 1965, I was out of sorts. It wasn't
homesickness per se—it was something else. I was lonely
for the company of someone my age. Actually, my fourteen-
year-old heart ached for someone to love.

I hadn't left a pining girlfriend back home in Blacksburg, though I wish I had. I'd sent postcards to several
friend-girls, hoping my Continental exposure would im-
press, keeping the whole story to myself, of course.

My heartache was not just a function of time and distance. As soon as we landed in Luxembourg, my psyche
was stoked by a daily assault of feminine sensuality in a
foreign land. Then Paris amped it up as if the city were
destined to grow my libido, feeding it in the streets, in
sidewalk cafés, and even in the museums like the Louvre,
where naked women graced canvas or personified marble
everywhere you looked. And it didn't help that my parents
let us see James Bond seduce Pussy Galore in *Goldfinger*
in a theater on the Champs-Élysées. And in the biggest
shock of my young life, Dad exposed our whole family to

the Folies Bergère. Then came the nymph-prone country-side of France and Switzerland, followed by the models of Milan, who sat sidesaddle in short skirts on the back of Vespas, hugging the appreciative waists in front of them. More torturous paintings and statues nourished me in Rome. And then, in Pompeii, I was declared old enough for the "men only" viewing of two-thousand-year-old erotic frescos that adorned the walls of an ancient brothel, since excavated from Vesuvius's entombing volcanic ash and scorching young eyeballs to this day.

◆ ◆ ◆

By the time we got to Florence, I was a tornado of hormones that sent me on a mission to find somebody to love. And there, right in the café attached to our campground, I found her.

The owner of the campground lived with his family in a villa attached to the front gate. He worked in the office, and his wife and three daughters helped in the adjoining café with a limited menu of coffee, mineral water, sodas, breadsticks, and pastries. My sisters and I were thrilled to learn that Coca-Cola came in a six-ounce glass bottle with a *real* straw, a golden grainless shaft that turned every ounce sucked into instant foam. We would sit around a table, commiserating about our parents, cutting up, and laughing. The owner's daughters were about our age, and if there were no other customers, they would sit at a table across the room and do likewise, as if we were in a sibling competition of goodwill and frivolity. But I wasn't concentrating on wit. The middle daughter drew all my attention.

She was beautiful beyond anyone I'd seen that summer. She peered at me with big brown eyes blinking beneath the part of her long, dark hair. She would smile, avert her gaze, giggle, look back at me, and smile again, looping a finger around her ear to gather strands of hair that never looked out of place to me. She looked like someone Leonardo da Vinci wished he could have painted. I fell in love. Over the next few days, I manufactured every excuse I could to go to the office or the café to catch a glimpse of her. I ordered more Cokes than my budget could stand, fantasizing that she would come and sit with me. And then, one afternoon, she did. She joined me with her Coke and straw, a sign that I took to mean we were meant for each other. We smiled and laughed and produced Coke foam too fast, erupting in coughs and laughter that made me love her even more. We traded words in English and Italian by pointing at things, but mostly, we got lost in each other's smiling eyes. Her sisters alternated keeping watch, and after a while, her father came and said something to her that made her frown, sigh, and rise from our table. But as much as I hated seeing her go, I knew that we had already reached our end. Our inability to communicate fully and my pending departure settled its heaviness on my heart and, I think, on hers too.

Before she left the room, she turned and gave me one last smile, blew me a kiss, and was gone.

But she has never disappeared.

Life Lessons
- Teenage hormones explain why human beings are still walking the earth.
- Some enchanting moments can last as long as your memory.

DAD'S ILLNESS: PART I

One day in second grade, when I came home, two men I didn't know were in the family room talking to my mother. When she saw me, Mom asked me how school was. The men said hello like they knew me. Mom got me a snack in the kitchen. Then, she rejoined the men in the den, where they spoke in whispers. A little later, Mom invited me to join them.

"Richard," Mom said, looking at me with watery eyes. "Your father is in the hospital." She added other assurances like "He'll be all right" and "Don't worry." And I didn't worry because I'd been taught that hospitals were places people went to get well.

◆   ◆   ◆

Over the next few months, life went on, but things were different. Dad wasn't around at all. Mom cried a lot. She missed Dad. We all did.

I remember driving to Radford with Mom and my sisters so Mom could visit Dad in the hospital. Radford had two hospitals. Sometimes, I went with Dad to the other hospital, where he visited sick church members. I had to wait in the lobby because I wasn't yet twelve years old. I had never seen this hospital. Mom called it a special hospital. It was quieter than the other one, red brick, surrounded by trees, and overlooking the New River. There weren't many people coming and going. We kids stayed in the car in the parking lot. Mom wasn't gone long. When she returned, we could tell she'd been crying again.

While Dad was in the hospital, we visited Mom's parents a lot in Mount Airy, North Carolina. My grandmother's cookie jar was always filled with her homemade sugar cookies, and one time while sneaking in to get another one, I heard my mother arguing with her older sister about Dad. My aunt said Mom should leave him; it was the smart thing to do. I hated that aunt for years.

Dad came home a month or so later. He was tired and slow. But after a while, he got better.

The next summer, Mom took courses to get her teaching certificate. Her first assignment was at Price's Fork Elementary and later, at Blacksburg High School. She taught school until she retired.

Many years later, I learned that the two men in the living room with my mother had been church deacons to help her admit Dad to St. Albans Hospital to treat his clinical depression. His therapy included electric shock treatments, now known as electroconvulsive therapy, which had worked well for him when he was hospitalized in North Carolina before I was born. Mom started teaching as a backup plan should Dad no longer be able to pastor a church. The people of Blacksburg Baptist Church were supportive throughout his illness and recovery.

It would not be the last time.

Life Lessons
- Even fathers can get sick.
- Some family secrets can stay buried for a long time.

LOST IN ROME

Dad, Mom, my sisters, and I reached our campground in Rome near dusk. Our tent site was in a pine forest atop a hill overlooking the 1960 Summer Olympic stadium. As I looked down on the ruddy track, my mind could see Wilma Rudolph winning her gold medals on that surface. I could hear the crowd's roar, just as it did in the famous ancient Coliseum that I knew must be out there somewhere under the setting sun. So, when Dad suggested that after we pitched our tent and ate a bite of supper, we drive into the city and take in the sights of Rome at night, I was all in. My sisters were too. Mom decided to stay home and turn in early—another confirmation of her maternal wisdom.

Finding the Coliseum was so easy that I wondered if "all roads lead to Rome" was actually true. We walked through the Coliseum's shadows and gazed into the reflective eyes of hundreds of cats that lived there. This was our lucky night, or so we thought.

We didn't know until later that being in the Coliseum at night could be dangerous.

We drove farther, marveling at plazas, fountains, architecture, bridges, and the incredible Roman Forum. We made our way into the Plaza of the Vatican and saw St. Peter's Cathedral illuminated by a battery of spotlights. It was such a stunning and moving sight that we decided our night of exploration should end on that spiritual high, and we turned to head home.

The problem was that while we had a general sense of direction of where our campground might be, we lacked specifics. Decades before cellular phones and GPS, we depended on maps, and the map Dad picked up at the campground office was lacking. The wondrous Roman streets that had funneled us into the city's center morphed into a cobblestone cobweb. Worse, the campground's name was ensconced in the pocketbook and mind of that day's navigator: Mom.

As we soon learned, all roads do not lead to Rome—at least not the places you actually want to go.

We were lost. I am at a loss in my attempt to convey how lost we were. We went to parts of Rome that I remain certain no Americans had ever visited. We nearly wedged our Microbus in one narrowing dead-end alley after another. Dad tried to get directions to the Olympic Stadium near our campground from so many people that we lost count. No one spoke English. All policemen seemed to be on holiday. We found one helpful individual who spoke French, which helped a little bit, but he ran out of fingers, threw up his hands, and said to my father, "Mister, it is very difficult!"

My father went into several bars, the only things open, to find anyone who might help us. Being lost is exhausting, and my little sister and I began to nod off.

My older sister, Carol, told me the next morning that when Dad was trying to stop in front of a bar where a row of motorcycles and scooters stood side by side, he misjudged his approach and knocked over the first motorcycle, which knocked over the second, until all of them fell to the pavement like dominoes. And Dad zoomed off; he didn't stop to apologize or offer to pay for damages, fearing for our lives.

Sometime past midnight, even Carol fell asleep.

When I woke up hours later, we were back at our tent.

The next day, Dad shared with us that he'd felt so helpless that night that as his children slept, he pulled over and broke down and cried. Then he prayed, "Please, God, help me find a way to get my family home." Soon thereafter, Dad stumbled upon our campground.

Postscript: I have always known that my father regretted his decision not to stop at the bar and apologize for hitting those bikes. But I also know the real reason he didn't stop is that he wanted to protect us; stopping might have put all his children in harm's way. I suspect that decision haunted him for the rest of his life.

Life Lessons
- Don't leave home without your home's address.
- When you are so hopelessly lost that you no longer know where you are going, try seeking your ultimate guide. You just might find your way.

UNCLE TEBO'S ADVICE

When I planned to go to Myrtle Beach with three guys during the summer before my senior year in high school, my father's brother, Tom, whose nickname was Tebo, suggested that I look up the daughter of a Presbyterian minister he knew there. I offered a polite "Sure. Thanks, Uncle Tebo!" But my mind was screaming, *Are you kidding me? Like we're going to need help with girls. And a preacher's daughter? Yeah, right.*

But after a few days of striking out on every overture our quartet made to any girl we thought might be living just for a chance to spend time with guys like us, I gave in and called the girl Uncle Tebo suggested. Jeannie Ann was pleasant on the phone as I explained our connection and how he made me promise to look her up. She invited us over right away, fed us cookies and iced tea, laughed at our buffoonery, and got dates for my friends, and we went together to the famous Beach Club that night, where we heard Jackie Wilson sing "Higher and Higher." We had a wonderful time.

The next summer, as I was marking days before matriculation at Wake Forest, Uncle Tebo sent me a note. He suggested I look up a girl he knew in Wilson, North Carolina, Janice Pope, who was also headed to Wake. This time I listened, and on the first day of freshman orientation, I marched down to Janice's dorm, introduced myself, and shared my relation to Uncle Tebo.

Four years later, two weeks after we graduated from Wake, Janice and I were married and have been ever since. Uncle Tebo sang at our wedding.

In the winter before our wedding, I confess that I let an excellent fraternity party affect my performance on the LSAT test that I took the following morning. When my disappointing scores arrived that jeopardized the probability of law school admittance, I sent a postcard to Uncle Tebo and asked him if he would tell me something about his profession of hospital administration, thinking it might be time to consider other alternatives.

My uncle Tebo took the time to send me a single-spaced, five-page letter about how his work was the perfect combination of service and business, science and art, architecture and politics, and management and leadership. His eloquence and sincerity encouraged me to look into health administration. I applied to Duke, his alma mater, and I know that his recommendation to the graduate program helped with my admission. Along my career path, I consulted Uncle Tebo several times about the pros and cons of the jobs I was considering. His advice and counsel were tremendous gifts that helped me in my forty-two-year career as a healthcare executive.

I thanked Uncle Tebo several times, once in a letter that included retelling him the events written here, thanking him for his role in the advent of my career and my marriage. When he got my letter, he was magnanimous and deflected any credit I gave him for my success.

After his death, his eldest son told me how much that letter meant to him. I was glad that I sent it, but I knew I could never thank him enough.

Life Lessons
- Some people don't listen to good advice until they run out of other options.
- Thank your mentors. It will mean more to them than you might imagine.

THE COLOSSUS OF ANOTHER
RHODES

During my tenure at Presbyterian Hospital in Charlotte, renovations were frequent. One project required that the main corridor connecting our largest parking deck to the rest of the hospital be shut down for twelve hours. The best alternative route was to detour thousands of people through our executive office suite to a back hallway. We decided to tackle this rerouting of ambulatory patients, visitors, guests, employees, and physicians on a weekday when more staff and volunteers would be on hand to assist.

On the morning that this pedestrian detour commenced at 7:00 a.m., I arrived early to find our staff ready with directional easels and signs that said, "Pardon our mess while we improve our facilities to better serve you." Smiles abounded as the temporary rerouting began. Observing from the doorway of my office, I saw that our first guests had no problems with the new route.

"Good morning, Mr. Howerton," our newly credentialed pet therapist said as she passed me.

"Good morning," I replied, smiling at her service dog, a large German shepherd, as it trailed obediently several feet behind her.

Then the dog stopped, raised its tail, squatted, pooped in the middle of the hallway, and trotted away. The pet therapist never saw a thing, and she and her professional canine turned onto the back hallway and out of sight before shock released my tongue. The therapy dog's steaming pile was an impressive heap.

Voices approached.

Guests are coming! I was the only staff member on the scene. There was no time to run for paper towels to clean it up, much less call housekeeping. But if the crowds tracked that stuff down the hall, the mess would grow, not to mention a publicity nightmare with no guilty hangdog on the scene. I had to act.

I walked to the steaming heap and straddled it, putting one polished dress shoe on its right and one on its left. No words of explanation for my stance or location seemed adequate, so I avoided making eye contact and stared straight ahead in rigid, stoic silence. As our visitors stepped to either side of me, my mind produced an image of that giant statue in ancient times that guarded a harbor—the Colossus of Rhodes.

When a lull in the traffic occurred, I ran to the bathroom, grabbed a wad of toilet paper, picked up the dog's leavings, flushed them, and called housekeeping. Someone had beaten me to it; they were already on their way. A little later, the horrified pet therapist came back to apologize and swear such a thing had *never, ever* happened before. The dog had no such mishap again during its many beneficial visits with our patients.

News of this event spread on the hospital grapevine all day. That afternoon my team gave me a new title to add to my resume: The Colossus of Poop. More hospital staff smiled at me that day than any I can remember.

Life Lessons
- Shit happens. And even if it's not of your making, sometimes you may be the one who has to clean it up.
- Sometimes, your only choice is to go with your gut instinct and stick to it.

THE FOLIES BERGÈRE

For some reason, Dad decided that our trip to Paris would not be complete without a visit to the famous Folies Bergère. We put on our Sunday best to visit that historic performance venue, which was nearing its hundredth year of operation. From what my parents had described, I imagined we'd see some dumb comics and silly vaudeville routines, perhaps a good cancan number.

Maybe that's what we would have seen in the late nineteenth century. But this was 1965.

Dad bought tickets that put us on the first row of the mezzanine with a perfect view of the stage and a yard away from the suspended catwalk that arced along the edge of our balcony. The show included singers, dancers, and comedians, one of whom used a trampoline in his act about a fearful high diver. And there were plenty of dancers in fancy plumed costumes, all as expected.

The amount of nudity was a surprise.

Right before my fourteen-year-old eyes, along that catwalk only three feet away, paraded dozens and dozens of showgirls wearing only high heels and rhinestone

G-strings below bouncing and swaying breasts adorned with glittering pasties. I could not believe that my Southern Baptist preacher father had placed me in that prime seat of proximity, but there was no way I would ask him why he put me in my current position of heaven on earth. I teetered between extreme titillation of what I beheld and the expansive hydraulic discomfort in my loins resultant thereto. I lost a few IQ points permanently that night; my brain was damaged from lack of transported oxygen by the blood that pooled where it did for two hours. The Adam and Eve in the Garden of Eden skit about killed me. When the show was over, I could hardly walk.

What my father expected or hoped to impart to us on that visit to the Folies Bergère, I will never know. My sisters and I have regaled in telling others about our time at the Folies Bergère, but I can't remember our parents ever discussing it with us. Perhaps Dad, as a lover of art, wanted to see the place that impressionists Édouard Manet and Henri de Toulouse-Lautrec had painted more than a few times. Or perhaps Dad wanted us to experience something that only could be experienced in Paris. Or perhaps he wanted to expose us to a part of life outside museums, cathedrals, castles, a place filled with song, laughter, and, yes, the beauty of artistic expression, costumed or not.

Perhaps—a thought that occurred to me years later—he simply had no idea what he was getting us into.

I wish I had asked him.

Life Lessons
- Know exactly where you're taking your family (and what you'll find when you get there).
- Ask your parents all the questions you can while they are still on this earth.

CAT SCRATCH FEVER

Our first child, Seth, was born at Portsmouth Naval Hospital, and he was six weeks old when we left him with a babysitter for the first time. It was a big deal. We'd been invited to a party of fellow Navy Medical Service Corps officers and their spouses. Janice got references on babysitters and selected the most recommended one a few houses down the street. Our next-door neighbors, Walton and Nancy, had three children, and Janice made sure that they would be home and on call as a backup.

Their "great babysitter" references notwithstanding, we were nervous. Seth was a demanding soul, and whenever anything startled him, he would wail and screech in a tone and volume that could shatter eardrums. When our babysitter showed up with a friend, another girl her age, we thought we were getting two helpers for the price of one. Janice gave them an extensive orientation, including an introduction to our Balinese cat, Phoebe, who just had kittens that we'd recently sold. Making sure that we left the phone numbers of our host and neighbors, we departed on that beautiful, warm September evening feeling like we were on our first date of a new era.

◆ ◆ ◆

We were enjoying the company of friendly adults when our host came up to me and said, "Richard, you need to head home. Your neighbor called and something happened at your house with the babysitters. He said the baby is fine; don't worry."

We sped home, worrying all the way.

When we pulled into our driveway, Walton was standing on our front porch wearing his army flak jacket, jeans, and combat boots. Red rubber electric-shock-protection gloves made his hands look like huge Mickey Mouse paws.

We ran up to Walton and asked, "What happened?"

"Seth is fine. Your cat attacked the babysitters. They called me and then locked themselves in the bathroom with the long cord telephone."

"Oh no!" we said.

"When I got here, the stereo was turned way up, and Phoebe was hollering like a banshee. But I was prepared," he said, nodding to his getup and hoisting his red rubber gloves. "My guess is Phoebe was trying to protect Seth."

"Thank you so much, Walton!" I said.

"But what did Phoebe do?" Janice asked.

"That's the thing. Phoebe scratched the babysitter wearing short shorts on her virgin inner thigh. But don't worry. Knowing how bad cat scratch fever can be, I went ahead and sucked all the venom out."

Oh, my God! Did he really?

After a three-second pause, Walton doubled over with deep guffaws. I couldn't help but laugh too, wondering if things would turn out all right. A cat scratch on a fourteen-year-old thigh could be a major problem. *We could get sued!*

Janice swabbed the babysitter's wounds with alcohol while I fretted whether our homeowner's insurance would cover us for our cat permanently scarring a young female thigh.

Janice called the babysitter's mother to apologize and offer to pay any medical bills.

The girl's mother, who happened to be a veteran nurse and an operating room supervisor, told Janice, "Don't you worry, hon. Those dumb girls probably got what they deserved."

Life Lessons

- It's good to have a babysitter with an understanding mother.
- Great neighbors are priceless.

BARNSTORMER

One evening, my mother and I were alone in the kitchen, disagreeing about something. My know-it-all teenage pontifications made Mom clang pots with more vigor than usual.

Mom commenced *pshew*-ing between the sink and dishwasher, a sign that her ire was nearing full boil. If I were younger, she might've warned, "The red flag's going up!"—a sure sign that it was high time to change whatever course I was pursuing. But that night, I was not deterred. In response to something she said, I declared, "Mom, you are *so boring!*"

Mom whipped around, leaned forward, and demanded, "Have *you* ever been barnstorming?"

Her non sequitur shocked me into silence. From old movies I'd seen on TV, I knew that barnstorming was when pilots of open-cockpit biplanes landed in farmers' fields and sold rides to local thrill-seekers, which often included zooming down toward a barn only to pull up at the last minute. It's not something I imagined my mother ever doing, and as she already knew, it wasn't something I'd ever done.

Before I could make another smart-aleck remark, Mom said, "Well, I have!" Then she turned her back to me as if that proclamation would be enough to end our conversation. And it was.

◆　◆　◆

On the next Sunday morning, sitting next to Mom in a church pew, I tried to picture her in a biplane cockpit behind her boyfriend doing airborne loops, dives, and stalls versus sitting here now, passing the offering plate after Dad's sermon. I'd learned that Mom not only went barnstorming with a local pilot, but he was also her high school boyfriend and had asked her to marry him. Had Mom picked a dashing barnstormer over a serious preacher, I wouldn't have been born.

I then realized just how little I knew about Mom's life before my mind perceived her as my mother.

Life Lessons
- You never know what lives your parents lived before you came around.
- Mothers often get the last word.

ANGEL ON FIFTH AVENUE

The morning after I dined in New York City with my childhood girlfriend and her husband, I woke up in a deep funk.

Dinner the evening before had been delightful. We ate in Greenwich Village at the Knickerbocker, listening to jazz and drinking too much wine. I had never met her husband, and I wasn't surprised that he was a great guy. Just before midnight, we traded bittersweet hugs and said our goodbyes. Back in my Midtown hotel room, I didn't sleep much, rethinking how it was my fault that we had not spoken for years.

A few months back, as I mentioned in a previous story, I had surprised her by calling to say I was sorry that my actions had terminated our long and special friendship. She was a magnanimous listener, with a scant recollection of the specific circumstances that burdened me with years of guilt and regret. She forgave me, and I was happy to receive her forgiveness. Now, in the light of dawn, I felt a heaviness descend and blanket my awareness that I had denied myself the good times that might have been.

I went to the morning session of the healthcare seminar that had brought me to the city, but my thoughts were elsewhere. At noon, I traded lunch for fresh air. Wandering up and down Fifth Avenue, I kept pace with the crowd, oblivious to the scenery and the river of human beings carrying me along in its flow. A crossing light flashed a red "DON'T WALK," and I stood on the curb of a street with no one in front of me. The crowd collected beside and behind me in a cocoon of humanity. When the crossing light changed to a white "WALK," I stepped forward automatically into the street.

Suddenly, I was yanked back. Something, no . . . some*one* had pulled me back by the collar of my coat. *Who did that?*

Then a blast of air hit me as a massive step van zoomed by. Had I taken that step, I would have been crushed, flattened, or splattered.

The shock of that realization froze me where I stood. With the street ahead now empty, the crowd surged forward, parting around me. I turned to thank the person who had probably saved my life by their gracious act.

There was no one there.

Life Lessons
- Don't let thoughts of what might have been keep you from seeing what's right in front of you.
- Whether or not you believe in guardian angels, pay attention while walking the streets of New York City.

MY BIG SISTER'S TEETH

One night, my older sister, Carol, woke up, went to the bathroom, fainted, and knocked out her two front teeth on the edge of the bathtub. Dad rushed her to our dentist, who advised permanent replacements should wait until adulthood, as was the practice at the time. Thus, throughout her teen years, Carol endured a temporary plate, to which she rendered faithful brushings every morning and night and on special occasions like going to church or shopping.

The night of Carol's first date was one such occasion.

Carol, Mom, and Sarah Jane twittered with possibilities of what she should wear, how to fix her hair, and how she should act on a proper first date. All the fuss seemed dumb to me, but when I shared that opinion, I was told that I was too young to understand and didn't know what I was talking about since I was just a silly little brother. I was miffed, so much so that when I walked by Carol—about to give her real teeth a final brushing—and spied her false teeth in the sink, I snatched them and ran.

Until that point, I viewed Carol as a kind, thoughtful, intelligent human being who wouldn't hurt a fly. While I had aggravated her to the point of anger many times, I had never heard her raise her voice. I was expecting, "Now, Richard, be a good boy and bring my teeth back. Pretty please."

What I got was a wild woman. She screeched and gave chase. As we circled the kitchen table, she grabbed Dad's carving knife, raised it over her head, and shouted, "Give them back!"

I did.

Life Lessons

· False teeth and first dates are never to be trifled with.

· Everyone has a breaking point.

HAIL THE QUEEN

When Janice and I moved as newlyweds to Durham, North Carolina, for my graduate school stint at Duke, we had the great fortune of moving into an apartment across from Jill and Tom Ristine. We became friends for life. After Duke, Jill and Tom returned to Indianapolis, where they invited us to attend the greatest spectacle in sports: the Indianapolis 500. After experiencing this unique event with Tom several times, I dreamed of taking my kids someday, and when Seth turned twelve and Drew was ten, we made plans to go.

Race day arrived on a beautiful Indiana day. Jill and Janice decided to stay home with too-young Rob and the fabulous Ristine daughters. Tom, Seth, Drew, and I journeyed to the Indianapolis Motor Speedway, where over three hundred thousand fans tried to find parking spaces. Tom shunned several paid lots near our Sixteenth Street approach to the speedway, choosing instead to zigzag his minivan through adjacent neighborhoods in search of a free space. He selected a spot on the side of a neighborhood street where no other cars were parked. We gathered our gear and headed toward the speedway.

As we neared Sixteenth Street and its teeming race traffic, I had a premonition that I needed to say something to my sons about what they might be exposed to in the next few hours, like my father might have wondered before he took my sisters and me to the Folies Bergère. Unlike Dad, I chose to say something.

"Now, boys, you are about to see and hear things that I don't want to ever see you do or hear coming out of you. Do you understand me?"

Both sons looked at me as if I were a paternal alien intent on stealing their good life, but they had the sense to say, "OK, Dad. Whatever."

We carried on, walking across a parking lot that bordered an old clapboard house surrounded by motorcycles. An Indiana chapter of the Hells Angels had made that house its race-day home. Club members were coming and going between the house and two long sofas that they'd hauled to the edge of Sixteenth Street to view the passing cars. The sofas were packed with Angels.

There was a constant stream of pedestrian fans on the Sixteenth Street sidewalk, and we merged in among them and walked toward a railroad overpass bridge. This decline gave the sofa Angels an elevated view over our heads as we passed before them. To my sons walking in front of me, I whispered, "Eyes straight. Keep walking. Don't say a word."

Then, the Royal Court of the Indianapolis 500, its queen and princesses, perched and waving from their ceremonial convertibles, began to motor by. And when they did, the first sofa of Angels stood up, raised their beers, and in unison shouted, "Hail the queen! Hail the queen!" The first sofa hailers sat down, and the second sofa of Angels rose, raised their beers, and yelled, "F*** the queen! F*** the queen!" These alternating chants continued, echoing within the street's concrete cave until we climbed up and out of earshot.

I looked down at my sons and couldn't decide if their faces bore looks of astonishment or terror.

But our race day exposures didn't end there. Over the next four hours, my boys experienced:

1. topless women dancing on the roofs of RVs,
2. a flyover of US fighter jets,
3. thirty-three open-wheeled race cars zooming around at 220 miles per hour,
4. a lonely vacant space where Tom's minivan was supposed to be after the race, and
5. a ride in a police car to the lot where Tom's car was driven after it was discovered still running from its hot-wired start minus its Alpine radio.

After the lot attendant told my sons that it would be against the law to show them how to start a car with a screwdriver, he did exactly that.

It was a big day—the greatest spectacle in sports, I reckon.

Life Lessons

- You never know what you'll see at the Indy 500.
- Every generation has the potential to shock others with what they consider entertainment.

DAD'S ILLNESS: PART II

In August of 1968, I was home for lunch between my two-a-day high school football practices when Mom came in and said, "I need you to drive me to the airport tonight to pick up Dick."

Her statement was unusual. Normally, she would go by herself or send my older sister or me alone to pick up my father, but Carol was traveling between her college years, leaving only me to help if two of us were truly necessary for such a simple task. And to such superfluousness, usually I would protest that football practice rendered me useless for anything other than lying on the sofa and watching TV. But Mom's words sounded strange, serious, and fragile, as if she were handing me a cut glass vase of such delicacy that, without her hushed tone, it would shatter at my touch. Something was wrong.

After supper, I drove Mom from Blacksburg down into the scenic Roanoke Valley. It was still too light for the Star of Roanoke to be lit atop Mill Mountain. We spoke a few words; I may have been daydreaming about my upcoming senior year, which I expected to be the best of my life.

Last spring, I was elected president of the student council, and I'd returned a month ago from an all-expenses-paid trip to an inspiring national leadership conference in Hot Springs, Arkansas. I was looking forward to putting what I'd learned to work. Plus, for the first time in my football career, I was projected to be a starter.

I wasn't too concerned about whatever was going on with Dad. He was my hero. After years of enduring Dad's preaching from the pulpit every Sunday, lately I was beginning to enjoy my special status of being a PK, a preacher's kid. Church members often told me what a great preacher Dad was and how lucky I was to have him as a father, and I knew they were right. Dad taught me by sharing his thoughts, knowledge, and beliefs. He exposed me to things that none of my friends had experienced, like camping across the United States three times and in Europe for three months. He encouraged inquiry and discussion, and I reveled in challenging him to debates about random subjects, knowing that his limitless understanding of everything there was to know would prevail in the end.

Dad seemed to recall everything he had ever read, summoning on demand a poem from his teenage years as easily as something he'd absorbed last week. Since we were little, my sisters and I could win a dollar if we could find a word that Dad didn't know in the *Roanoke Times, Newsweek, Reader's Digest*, or any other nonscientific publication of our choosing, and we never won. Dad could talk to anyone on any level, from college professors to custodians to those who made their living off the land. He taught me to love nature's beauty, appreciate art and music, how to J-stroke a canoe, ride a horse, and rethink my positions when necessary. When my counterarguments deteriorated to spewing absurdities during our father-son debates,

Dad would pause and say, "You might want to rethink your position." That signal conveyed that I was ignorant about what I spoke of (i.e., full of crap), but somehow, it came across as encouragement to keep learning. Dad was a dreamer who shared his ideas about potential exploits that tried my mother's patience and her mathematician logic.

And then there were the opinions of girls and young women I knew; they loved him. Carol's friends gushed that our father was "so easy to talk to," a compliment conveying that his listening was on par with James Bond's debonairness. Taking advantage of my paternal asset, I would bring dates home, pretend I had forgotten something, and leave them with Dad, hoping that the warmth they felt for him would somehow transfer to me. It was as if Dad were an aphrodisiac of my hopeful intent that, when consumed, my dates could fathom the possibility of my transcending my current immaturity and growing up to be a chip off his sensitive, wise old block. If they didn't like Dad, they were soon history with me. Was I taking advantage of him? Of course, but Dad's love of people was sincere and heartfelt. He enjoyed getting to know people for who they were and who they might become, all as children of God. So how could my taking advantage of him be bad?

◆　◆　◆

When Mom and I reached Roanoke's Woodrum Airport, I parked, and we walked to the outside arrival gate and waited. We watched Dad's plane land and taxi, and after the Piedmont Airlines crew rolled the portable staircase into place, we walked through the gate's fence and out on the tarmac to greet him.

When Dad saw us, he stopped midway on the stairs and smiled, but his eyes were swollen, red, and bereft of joy.

When he got to Mom, he embraced her and began crying. He stood there for a long time, not letting her go, and he sobbed and sobbed. He may have looked at me once. I don't remember anything about our trip home or the rest of the night.

The next day after morning practice, Mom told me that Dad was in the hospital, and I wasn't surprised. When she told me that he was admitted to St. Albans, I didn't know what to think. St. Albans was a mental institution.

Later that evening, around the kitchen table, Mom explained to me and my little sister, Sarah Jane, that Dad was suffering another bout of his clinical depression like he had ten years before and a couple of times before that, all news to me. Mom said Dad needed treatment that eventually would make him well—electroshock therapy—but that was not something we needed to talk about in public.

Then Mom looked at me and said, "Richard, you are now the man of the house until your father gets better."

That was something I was not expecting to hear at that point in my seventeen-year-old life. But despite my unease, I felt pride at Mom's declaration, and that pride kept me quiet and still.

My conscious mind decided that I should and could be strong and carry on for the family, and we made a pact to keep our chins up. My subconscious mind had other ideas, but I was getting ahead of myself.

In September, school started. Other than a parade of visiting preachers substituting for Dad, our life kept its normal cadence as much as it could. But there was nothing normal about it.

Only one classmate asked me how I was doing.

"About what?"

"You know, about your dad."

"Oh, I'm fine. He'll be fine." Then I changed the subject.

In truth, I wasn't fine. I wanted the whole mess to go away. I was upset, but I decided to keep it to myself. I knew Dad couldn't help that he got sick; I wasn't stupid. What good would it do to get mad? In my mind's logic, it was silly to even *think* about the whole thing. "Just keep trying to act normal and let time pass" became my silent mantra— until I would erupt over the simplest things and lash out at Sarah Jane, who bore the brunt of my outbursts.

◆ ◆ ◆

One day, Dad came home, but not as the father I knew. He looked like himself, but he acted like someone I'd never met. He was dull, passive, lethargic, and distracted. I couldn't engage him in a conversation of more than a few words. He was there, but he wasn't. I hated whatever those doctors had done to him. It pained me to see my father that way, so I stayed away from him. We grew distant.

Mom held our household together. She communicated two things to me, loud and clear:

Just because Dad was sick didn't mean that I would get sick someday.

If I needed to talk with someone about this, she would make that happen.

Neither had occurred to me. I declined the offer of help and decided to have as much fun as possible, hoping that it would make my senior year pass as fast as possible. I couldn't wait to get away from home.

In about a year, Dad was himself again. It was as if his illness had never happened. Our old relationship returned, and I was thankful. I never talked with Dad about his illness. What good would it do to dredge all that up? So, I decided to pretend it never happened.

That decision came to haunt me, and years later—as you'll hear in a later story—it took its toll.

Life Lessons

· Sometimes, you can lose people when they're still around.

· Letting things go can be wise, but some things must be dealt with because you will live with them for the rest of your life, one way or another.

CINCINNATI

One evening in the last century, I was sitting in the family room of Janice's parents in the company of my teenage brother-in-law, Damon. We watched the boring offerings of primetime network television, hoping to find a more exciting show at ten o'clock. When Janice and my mother-in-law, Ruthmary, joined us, Damon turned up the volume out of respect for his mother's hearing.

Flipping through the channels, Damon discovered the opening credits of *The Love Boat*, which prompted him to express in a *hallelujah* tone of someone who just discovered a gold mine, "T and A!"

I chortled, knowing that that TV show delivered semi-exposed flesh moving under scant clothing with gratuitous frequency.

Then Ruthmary asked, "What does 'T and A' mean?"

My mind raced. If Damon answered truthfully, then it could spark mother-son trouble, to which I would be both a witness and a chortling accomplice. My status as a son-in-law in good standing with Ruthmary, with whom I had begun to share a risqué joke now and then, might protect me more than him. Plus, I was beginning to develop a special relationship with Damon that I wanted to grow.

Before Damon could answer, in the full presence of my wife, I decided to jump in and express to my mother-in-law the unfiltered truth of what "T and A" meant. Without prelude or further explanation, I said clearly, "It means tits and ass."

Ruthmary looked perplexed. Her brow wrinkled and shaded her squinting eyes. I feared that she was either doubting my judgment for expressing those words or Janice's judgment for marrying such a classless cad.

"Cincinnati?" Ruthmary asked.

After explaining our laughter to Ruthmary, she laughed along with us. From that day forward, the name of that great city in Ohio has been the family code for such sightings.

Life Lessons
- Some family members serendipitously invent a secret language to communicate and connect with one another.
- Humor in the face of misunderstandings is one hallmark of a great relationship.

COWBOYS AND INDIANS

In the summer of 1992, I drove Janice and our three sons "out West." We crossed the Mississippi River in Wisconsin and first spied the Great Plains in southern Minnesota. After a stop at Pipestone National Monument, where Indians had crossed the plains to its red cliffs of sandstone they carved into bowls for ceremonial pipes, four-year-old Rob began accumulating Indian gear. By the time we left the Badlands, Custer State Park, and the Crazy Horse Memorial, Rob had decked himself in a headdress and a buckskin vest and carried a bow and arrow, a rubber knife in a beaded sheath, and a feathered leather tomahawk.

Our first Wyoming destination was Cody, named for William "Buffalo Bill" Cody. We had reservations at the Irma Hotel, named for Buffalo Bill's daughter and famous for a gift from Queen Victoria: a mammoth bar of carved cherry, now the centerpiece of the Silver Saddle Saloon, the hotel's restaurant. We checked in before supper, unpacked, cleaned up, and changed. Rob took off his Indian paraphernalia and displayed his treasures on the top of the chest of drawers like a historic shrine. When I left to scout out the menu options downstairs, Rob tagged along. When Rob and I strolled into the Silver Saddle, we found the massive bar packed with locals. By locals, I don't mean merchants, brokers, and bankers; I mean cowboys. At first, I wondered if a troupe of actors for the staged gunfight in Main Street had taken a break. But no, these were *real* cowboys, the kind with dirty hats, fraying denim jackets, weathered jeans, leather boots scuffed to suede, and tooled belts suspending holstered revolvers. Elbows on the bar steadied their stern, unshaven faces so they could hover in silence over beer mugs and shot glasses. Eye contact seemed neither invited nor wise.

The hostess gave me a menu, and the entrées looked good; from her, I learned that the local cowhands had gathered at this same time and place for decades. We headed back upstairs to relay the finding of our reconnaissance to the rest of the family.

The second we entered our room, Rob began to stagger and stomp as if he were about to collapse after a shoot-out in a Western movie.

"Shoo wee! Oh man!" he said as he brushed his hand across his forehead and flicked sweat away in a show of extreme relief. He fell across the bed and moaned.

"What in the world is the matter, Rob?" Janice asked.

Rob replied, "I sure am glad I didn't wear my Indian stuff down *there!*"

Life Lessons
- Kids say the most honest things about what culture teaches them.
- Perception can be reality to a four-year-old (and many adults).

BICYCLE SUMMIT

Growing up as a twelve-year-old on a bicycle in the hills of Blacksburg, Virginia, was exhilarating and challenging. From the top of Kent Street, I could zoom down along the Virginia Tech campus at a velocity exceeding the speed limit. But biking up that same hill always defeated me, requiring I dismount and walk. But one Sunday afternoon, I made it all the way, reaching the summit, where I threw my hands up in victory, closed my eyes, and let the euphoria of my triumph waft over me.

Until I hit a parked car.

The first thing I remember was seeing green leaves and limbs against a clear blue sky. I felt warmth on my back, rising from the street's asphalt. Someone was moaning, making ghastly sounds sufficient to rouse the neighbors from afternoon naps. And then I realized those moans were coming from me.

Two women who made my grandmothers look young came to my aid. They assessed my injuries, picked me up, carried me into their house, and called my parents. They assured me that Mom and Dad were on their way and they would do what they could until they arrived. My pain possessed me so completely that I didn't object when those women pulled down my pants and put ice on my crotch where my testicles had attempted to merge with the junction of my bike's top tube and handlebars.

At the doctor's home office, I heard him say to my parents, "Your son will be fine. He should be able to reproduce someday. Time will heal the swelling, but I'm not sure about his pride."

Then the doctor came over to me. He winked and said, "And as for you. You keep your eyes open. And watch out for those parked cars."

Life Lessons

- Some pain can be so intense that you don't care who sees you naked.
- Your exuberance about an achievement should never stop you from keeping an eye out for what's right in front of you.

MARSHALL

Like many four-year-old kids, our son Rob had an imaginary friend. His name was Marshall, and Rob didn't care who heard his end of their conversations.

Sometimes, when Rob would laugh at what seemed like nothing, we'd ask, "What's so funny?"

"What Marshall said," Rob would reply as if that should have been obvious.

We didn't worry about our youngest son having an imaginary friend. Childhood experts and mothers' common knowledge told us they would go away soon enough. Nothing to worry about. Let the kid be a kid.

Even Rob's two teenage brothers tolerated Marshall. They refrained from making fun of Rob for his mind's vivid creation. Until one night, when Rob took it in his head to volunteer more specifics about Marshall around our dinner table.

"Marshall's a colored boy," Rob informed us.

The rest of his family pounced, firing quick retorts like "Rob, I can't believe you said that!" and "You can't say someone's colored" and "Why would you say such a

thing?" These reactions were consistent with our nondiscriminatory childrearing of all three sons.
Rob burst into tears. "But he *is* a colored boy!" he protested. "He has green hair, yellow eyes, an orange nose, and purple skin!"

Life Lessons

- You can count on a little kid to tell the literal truth.
- Harmless reality can sometimes seem discriminatory in another context.

WRONG BLOOD TRAGEDY

My sleep was light and restless when I was the administrator on call at Presbyterian Hospital, but the phone on my bedside table jolted me awake nonetheless. The night nursing supervisor said one of our cardiologists needed to speak to me right away.

After a pause of no more than a second, the physician came on the line and said, "Richard, you need to come in and tell my patient's family that your hospital gave him the wrong blood type. The mistake will likely kill him." Before I could ask anything, he added, "And you need to hurry. We can't keep him alive much longer, and it would be best for all of us if you tell his family before he dies."

The supervisor met me when I got to the hospital, and on our way up to the coronary care unit, I learned from her that a nurse, one of our best, had picked up a unit of blood from the blood bank and administered it to the wrong patient. Multiple errors were committed; our double checks had failed, and the oversights had sent an already compromised patient into an incompatibility reaction from which he would not recover. There was nothing else we could do for him. It should never have happened, but it was our fault, plain and simple.

Things happened fast, and though my mind searched through alternative actions, my gut told me that the physician's judgment was right—we needed to admit what happened and take responsibility for it. And tonight, that duty fell to me.

The patient's family was gathered in a conference room near the CCU. Pain creased the faces of his wife, his daughter, and four other friends and relatives. Their watery eyes and clenched teeth told me they knew something had gone wrong. The cardiologist introduced me, and I began to tell them about our hospital's mistake. I had received no training in what to say on a night like this, but I told the truth, took responsibility for what had happened, and expressed our sincere regret and sympathy.

My news collapsed their collective hope. One of them shouted, "No!" Another said, "This can't be happening. How could this happen?" Several broke down in tears, anger rose, and curses and condemnations followed. And they were justified.

Their husband, father, and friend died within thirty minutes.

◆ ◆ ◆

Throughout the rest of the night and into the next morning, there were notifications to be made, reports to be given, and investigations to get underway. The distraught wife of the patient called the local television station because she believed the public deserved to know what had happened. Later that afternoon, a health reporter interviewed me on camera for the evening local news. I expressed how our thoughts and prayers were with the family, how distressed our staff was that we, an institution whose mission it was to provide health care to our community, would be responsible for contributing to the death of one of our patients, and how we pledged to learn from this circumstance so that this mistake would not happen again in the future.

There were many difficult conversations and explanations with our staff, the public, and regulatory agencies in the coming days. The family's attorney accused us of initially covering up what happened, but the news reports, including my television interview, silenced that accusation. Our insurance company and hospital settled with the family for our tragic mistake.

All tough duty for me, those days and weeks proved to be, and while I've had other tough days since, nothing compares to speaking to that family. It remains the hardest thing that I have ever had to do in my life.

Life Lessons
- Admitting the truth, however bad, can be better than covering it up.
- The only good thing that can come from a tragedy is the knowledge and insight to prevent it from happening again.

FOOD FIGHT FRIENDS

Two of my hometown buddies were good friends, but when food entered the picture, at some point, more often than not, there would be a fight—a food fight.

It would start after they exchanged pleasantries. Time would pass, and then, without fanfare, one would look the other in the eye, grin, and say, "No! I won't let you." And it was time to take cover. In fairness, they targeted only each other, but their flung vittles would stray off course from time to time.

The rounds of their continuing food battles were many. I could regale you with the time that in the fanciest abode of our friends, they found the makings for a hamburger cookout in the kitchen and, at each other, they threw everything—lettuce, tomatoes, onion slices, and buns—and finished off with raw hamburger patties. Or I could share the time that Janice met my Blacksburg friends for the first time at a party after a Chicago concert when one of these two guys found a pickle in the bottom of his drink, and when the other laughed, war broke out with ammunition of drinks, crust cut off cucumber sandwiches, and

Fritos in a bowl the size of a snow-sledding saucer, followed by a quart of French onion dip. Janice hid behind the refrigerator to protect the white angora sweater her mother gave her for the occasion, where I am certain she pondered whether to reconsider someone with friends such as these.

But I *will* tell the time that one of my friend's girlfriends presented him with a homemade coconut layer cake—his favorite. It was a work of art, commanding the central spot for display on the kitchen counter of the apartment we rented that summer. When the other friend came by and saw it standing on a glass pedestal, tall and proud, he picked it up, walked over to the back of the couch where his antagonist sat, and asked, "How about a piece of cake?" To answer, my seated friend leaned his head back on the top of the couch, but before he could say a word, the cake arrived in his face via a motion not unlike an uncontested slam dunk. Hunks of that cake were thrown for the next twenty minutes until it was reduced to millimetric crumbs.

In all cases, these encounters would escalate until all edibles had been "consumed" in the launch, yet things never turned violent. Rather, following their fracas, these two food fighters would declare a cleaning armistice and get to work for as long as it took. They never asked for help (save for that one occasion our host's beagle helped by eating that raw hamburger off the kitchen walls). Their cleaning took hours, sometimes days. Special cleaning supplies had to be purchased on occasion; when the coconut flew, the walls and ceilings required new paint, all done with teamwork and in the peace of brotherhood.

Until next time.

Life Lessons
- If you make a mess, come together as a team, and do whatever it takes to clean it up.
- Some people just shouldn't eat together.

COUNTY CUTS

After returning home from a relaxing week at the beach with Janice and my two young sons, I settled down in the living room with a stack of local newspapers to catch up on what I'd missed. The front page of the *Burlington Times* read, "County to Eliminate Hospital Funding."

My breathing ceased. That was my hospital they were talking about.

Early the next morning, I learned that my staff had decided not to call me on my vacation about the county's intentions because they knew how much I needed to get away from the stress of serving as a hospital CEO in our demanding turnaround situation. After years of losses, we were almost breaking even, but our hospital remained dependent on county funding to finance its disproportionate share of charity care. The county's contribution equaled 5 percent of our total revenue, and if eliminated, we'd be back in red ink.

When I phoned my hospital board chair, he answered with a chuckle. "I've been expecting your call."

We were most fortunate to have Earl Pardue leading the Alamance County Hospital Board of Trustees. His business acumen had developed one of the most successful independent insurance agencies in the state, followed by diversification into real estate, investments, and thoroughbreds. He spread his service to our community broadly, but the main recipient of his eleemosynary dedication was County Hospital. Earl was a kind and gracious man with a keen sense of humor that smoothed over challenges and barriers that sometimes seemed insurmountable to me. After a dose of shared laughter with him, solutions came more readily. I knew he'd help me figure out this funding disaster.

◆ ◆ ◆

Earl suggested that we get on the county commissioner's meeting agenda the following night to plead our case, which he asked that I present. He would back me up, as I knew he would. He said he would pick me up for the meeting so we could chat on the way over.

The next night, when I took the lectern, I felt prepared, and I confess I believed I was persuasive in my arguments that the county should reverse its decision and reinstate our funding. I sensed I was on top of my public speaking game. When I finished, Earl stood up and endorsed what I said. There were few questions.

On the way home, Earl was effusive in his praise of my communication skill and the professionalism I had exhibited. I was starting to feel the warmth of pride welling in my chest.

"Thanks, Earl," I said. "That means a lot to me."

As he turned into my neighborhood, Earl added, "Yes siree, that was about the most impressive speech I have ever heard. Too bad it wasn't the least bit effective."

Several excruciating seconds passed before he burst into laughter.

Then he explained that it was clear that the county had made up its mind, and there was nothing that I could have said to change it. That's why no one had any questions for me. They were confident we could succeed without their funding, so they decided it wasn't needed. In a way, Earl said, he thought we ought to see it as a compliment to our leadership.

That got me laughing.

◆ ◆ ◆

The next day, our management team huddled and developed a plan to increase revenue, decrease costs, and communicate our actions to our board, employees, physicians, auxilians, and supporters, as well as the local newspaper and the county manager. Our trustees approved a revised annual budget. We communicated with all our publics that these actions would put our hospital on a sound footing for years to come.

At the end of that fiscal year, we exceeded our budget and had the best financial year in recent history.

Life Lessons
- Impressive does not mean effective.
- Humor can help clear your mind so you can tackle what needs to be done.

DAD'S ILLNESS: PART III

I hurried home after work from Portsmouth Naval Hospital, thinking I'd have time to mow the lawn before Janice got home from her teachers' meeting. I changed out of my summer white uniform into a T-shirt and cutoffs. On my way out, I paused to drink a tumbler of water in the kitchen when the wall phone rang.

It was Mom, and, as was her custom, she got right to the point. "Richard, your father is in the hospital," she said. Her voice told me that Dad's depression had struck again. She told me that Dad's Petersburg doctor had gotten him admitted to a good hospital in Richmond. I promised to visit her over the weekend.

Outside, my new Briggs and Stratton lawnmower started up with one yank of the pull cord. I made quick work of the front and side yards of the first house we owned and then hustled through our waist-high chain-link fence that enclosed our backyard. Pushing the mower with quick strides, I began my repetitive back-and-forth, a motion that usually brought me joy of visual accomplishment. But today, the grass's incessant growth and need for cutting infuriated me. No matter how well or often I cut it, it would only grow back and demand more chunks of my life. At the end of each swath, I rammed the mower until the fence's metal weave forced a full stop, then I yanked my stupid machine around, only to have to run the length of the yard again until I crashed once more into confining links of wire. The necessity of reversals, to-and-fros, and forced intermittent circumnavigation of trees and shrubs were maddening. *Why did the goddamn grass have to grow, anyway?*

At some point, I became aware of what I must have looked like. It was as if I were peering down from above and seeing a madman running behind a mower and using it to butt tree trunks and metal spans and posts, a man so out of control that he was swinging a running gasoline lawnmower around like an Olympic hammer thrower. *What in the hell is going on with that idiot? What is he . . . no, why is he . . . no, why am I acting so crazy?*

I stopped in the middle of the backyard and shut down the motor. With halting, unsteady steps, I made my way to our back stoop and sat down on the top step.

What just happened?

I took a deep breath and smelled the aroma of freshly cut grass that always smelled like watermelon to me. I gazed at the first lawnmower I ever purchased and saw its shiny silver and red carriage resting before its backdrop of tall uncut grass.

Mom's call. This all started after Mom's call. About Dad. Sick again.

When I saw Dad a few weeks ago, he seemed fine and happy in his last pastorate before his retirement. But now, his recurring disease and its bedeviling effects would transform his mind's proactive genius into indecisive lethargy. I knew Dad would get better slowly after a course of shock therapy and months of inertia. He always had. But he would not be the man I knew and loved for months and months. I knew he would get better. So why was I acting so crazy? Why was I so out of control? So full of . . . rage?

◆ ◆ ◆

Rage. I had heard that word before to describe me.

Two years ago, my therapist told me that I harbored enormous internal rage. He said those words in our last session together before I graduated from Duke and began my uniformed service obligation in the Navy Medical Service Corps. I had met him eighteen months earlier, after only four months as a newlywed. We'd moved to Durham, and two months into grad school, one morning after Janice left to teach elementary school to support us, I started crying. I didn't know why I was crying, but I could not stop for a long time. All I wanted to do was quit everything and do something different. A few hours later, I walked into the office of Dr. Jon Jaeger, the head of my health administration program, and told him that I wanted to drop out of school. He asked me a simple question: "Why?" I had no answer for him. Dr. Jaeger shared that he needed to talk to someone from time to time when he was "down and depressed." He suggested I, too, might benefit from talking to someone, and after I did, if I still decided to leave school, then he would help me move on to whatever I wanted to try next.

Since I didn't know why I wanted to quit and had nothing better to do, I said I would talk with someone, but "not a psychiatrist." Dr. Jaeger called and made an appointment for me for that afternoon. The therapist asked me how I was feeling, and I told him I felt nothing. Nothing. Not a thing.

After agreeing to set up another appointment the next day, I returned to our apartment and waited for Janice. She, my still-new bride, listened in stunned silence as I told her about my uncontrollable tears, my almost quitting school, my appointment with the therapist, my inability to feel anything, and my suspicion that since I couldn't feel anything about anything or anybody anymore, I must not feel love for anyone, maybe even for her.

The next day, when I relayed what I'd said to Janice, my therapist told me, honest or not, that had been such a cruel thing to say. Janice was indeed crushed. She didn't understand or know what to do to help me, but she stuck by me. She even went with me a few times to the therapist, but she and he knew soon that the problem resided in me, so I started sixteen months of weekly visits alone with him. It was a long, hard slog of confusion, doubt, and confession. I held on to the knowledge that I had been the happiest I had ever been in my life the day Janice said she would marry me, and I wanted to find that euphoria again. It had to be in me somewhere.

Slowly, things began to improve. My feelings of love for Janice emerged from the dark place where they'd been hiding. I began to thrive in school. Janice stood by me through the toughest year of our marriage, and our love prevailed. So, just when I had made it through school and was about to start a new chapter in our life story, I did not understand why my therapist would insist, on my last visit with him, that I was still full of hidden, inner rage that I had to get in touch with and work through because it wouldn't just go away—it would return. He urged me to find another therapist wherever we moved. But I had nothing of it. With proud intent, I told him that I thought he was full of shit. Couldn't he see that I was doing well? Oh, sure, I had been down, but I was doing just fine now, thank you very much.

◆　◆　◆

Yet now, here I was, sitting on my back stoop looking out over my half-mown lawn and wondering if what I told my therapist was true, what in the world was my wild mower man tantrum all about? If it happened right after Mom's call, then was I mad that Dad was depressed again? Why would anyone get angry about someone who couldn't help it when they got sick? I couldn't be angry at the father I loved for an illness he couldn't control, could I? What kind of asshole son would do that? Yet there it was, as plain to see as the gouges in the bark of the trunk of our magnificent elm tree. I sat, listening to the sounds of tires on asphalt as neighbors returned home and the buzz of insects flitting among petals.

Suddenly, something clicked. My father was last hospitalized for his depression when I was seventeen. I chose to ignore it and act like everything was normal. At Mom's declaration, I pretended to be "the man of the house" and refused the need to talk to anyone about what was happening. Suppressing whatever feelings I had, I decided to wait it out. I was told Dad would come home well. But then Dad returned as a different person, and I hated that version of him. And I buried that too, deep within the recesses of my being, where it resided and festered until choosing to erupt today. I recognized my enormous internal rage for the first time, as if it were saying, "I'm back—just try to ignore me this time!"

"Jesus Christ," I said to the sky. "I am angry that Dad got sick and left me. What a selfish prick. Lord, help me."

Something lifted off my shoulders as if I'd been carrying a hundred-pound sack of grain that I didn't know was there. I looked up and the sky's blue brightened.

Janice would be home soon. I couldn't wait to tell her what had just happened.

Life Lessons
- If you bury your feelings too deeply, they might erupt someday.
- An epiphany about the past doesn't mean you don't have a lot more work to do in the future.

GET DOWN

One evening while visiting Janice's parents, we had enough time to get baths for our young sons before her parents' friends from California stopped by. The visiting couple used to live in Wilson, North Carolina, where they became lifelong friends with Bob and Ruthmary.

After their baths, our sons, Seth and Drew, then six and four, donned their shorty Disney character pajamas and ran down the steps, eager to see the army uniforms we had told them about. We urged their best behavior since our visitors were now high-ranking officers in the Salvation Army. It was to be a friendly and proper visit.

Drew hopped up on the love seat next to me and sat with his legs crossed. Introductions and small talk ensued.

A few moments later, Drew raised his palm and smacked himself in the crotch. Then he did it again. And before anyone could stifle their shock and incredulity enough to ask what in the world he was doing, he hit himself again, looked down toward his lap, and shouted, "Get down, penis! Get down!" Then Drew leaned back, his face glowing from his apparent success.

Everyone took a breath, and then our friendly and proper conversation kept rolling along.

Life Lessons
- Nature can call at awkward times.
- Sometimes it's best to pretend it never happened and just keep talking.

FOLLOW YOUR BLISS

One night when I was thirty-seven, I was saying good-night to my oldest son, Seth, when he volunteered that he didn't know what he wanted to do when he grew up.

I had seen Bill Moyer's interview with Joseph Campbell for the PBS series *The Power of Myth*, and it had a profound effect on me. It inspired me to tackle Campbell's *The Hero with a Thousand Faces*, in which he wrote that myths and legends with similar themes arise independently from diverse cultures around the world to reveal fundamental truths. Heroes often follow similar steps in what Campbell called a "hero's journey." Campbell advised that humans should "follow your bliss" because in so doing, they rise to their highest potential. But Campbell's bliss was far removed from the pursuit of simple pleasure or escapism. Rather, it professed the wisdom that one becomes one's best self by acting to serve others before serving oneself. As a father of three young sons, I latched on to "follow your bliss" with the fervor of a sacred epiphany.

Sitting at Seth's bedside, I shared Campbell's philosophy and told him how wise I thought it was. Then I asked him, "Have you ever heard the proverb, 'Find a job doing what you love, and you'll never have to work a day in your life'?"

"Maybe," Seth said.

"'Follow your bliss' is like that. So, if you truly follow your bliss, do for a living what brings you great joy and allows you to be your best self, then you will know you are on the right track."

◆　◆　◆

Since then, my three sons have grown into good men, and they are each successful in their own way. I am proud of them. But my sons often made decisions about their lives that were different from what I recommended and wanted them to do. My bliss wasn't necessarily their bliss, nor their bliss mine. And in my weakest and most frustrating moments, I confess that I wished I had never thrust this Campbell bliss shit upon them in the first place.

But after a while, I would settle down and take another step along my journey of trying to follow my bliss and act more like a hero now and then.

Life Lessons
- Leaves on the same branch of a family tree grow differently, even with the same nurture and fertilizer.
- You can't take back the lesson once it's been taught.

COACH CLAIBORNE

As a teenager, I had the opportunity to meet Jerry Claiborne, then the head football coach at Virginia Tech. Coach Claiborne was a deacon at Blacksburg Baptist Church, my father's pastorate. I saw him there many Sundays, and I got to play softball with him while practicing for our church's summer league teams. He was a wonderful human being.

On one occasion, I heard Coach Claiborne say that he was headed to a national meeting attended by other football coaches from around the country. I asked him what coaches do at a national coach convention.

"We enjoy each other's company," Coach Claiborne said, "and we attend clinics, share and debate offense and defensive schemes, plays. Things like that."

That struck me as strange. Why would a coach share information with a potential competitor? I asked him, "You mean you actually teach coaches that you might compete against how to play better?"

"Yes," Coach Claiborne answered.

The look on my face must have conveyed how foolish I thought it was to help your competitors, because he placed his hand on my shoulder, looked me in the eye, and said, "Success is not about secrets, son. In the end, it's all about execution."

Life Lessons
- Tactics are important in the short run, and strategy is critical for the long run. Both require excellent execution to achieve success.
- Great teachers take time to teach whenever the opportunity presents itself.

INTOXICANT LOVE

The day that Janice Ruth Pope said she would marry me was the happiest of my life. Our three-year courtship was complicated with hometown loves and punctuated with mountaintop experiences, valleys of separation, testing and sharing, and the sweetest time with another human being I had ever experienced. When she said yes, my euphoria consumed all of my rational capacity and rendered me incapable of doing anything other than wanting to be with her and talk about our future.

During this exuberant time, I was enrolled in a class of legendary difficulty in my college major: politics. Dr. Richard Sears, an expert in the Soviet Union, was the most feared professor in the department. Known as a no-nonsense guy, his wit was Sahara dry. His lanky frame lofted a countenance of Cold War sobriety. Beneath his pate of receding hair, dark eyes darted in search of someone suitable to call on but rarely found one who proved worthy. Fellow students dreaded his highly-recommended-but-near-mandatory class. It was a trial of perseverance, a rite of political passage.

Janice accepted my proposal two days before I was to take Dr. Sears's dreaded midterm exam. My intoxicating love consumed me so that I decided my best hope was to go to see Dr. Sears, confess my addiction, and throw myself upon his mercy. "Hopeless odds for success" was the consensus among all with whom I shared my desperate plan.

The day before the midterm, I found Dr. Sears in his office behind his desk. He asked me what I wanted.

"Dr. Sears, I just got engaged, and I'm so happy that I can't do anything. I am in love beyond all reason. I cannot think. Is there any chance I could get a delay on my midterm?"

Dr. Sears leaned back in his chair and stared at me. He shook his head, and I prepared for the worst. Then he chuckled and turned to stare out of the window behind him. When he turned toward me, he smiled and said, "I remember that same feeling when I got engaged. Clearly, you would not be at your best. How does next week sound?"

Life Lessons
- Everyone has their own story—and that story may work to your advantage.
- It never hurts to ask.

MY FATHERLY PROM DATE ADVICE

When Rob was a sophomore at the Paideia School in Atlanta, he decided to go to his prom by himself. To Janice and me, this was a new concept. During our high school years, people didn't attend prom without a date—it was a permanent, inviolate rule. While we knew that young people went out in groups these days, going solo to a prom seemed too novel.

But Janice knew something that I didn't about this prom dilemma. She volunteered in the office at Paideia—a ploy she'd put into action at all our sons' schools—and there, she'd become aware of all kinds of things. In this case, she picked up that there was a senior girl, Suzanne Jones (not her real name), who wished Rob would take her to prom. Janice asked me if I would take one more shot at convincing Rob to get a prom date, man to man, by suggesting he ask Suzanne.

I found Rob in the basement playing video games, and I asked him if we could chat before supper.

"What's up?" Rob asked.

I tried to ease into things. "So, I hear you plan to go to the prom."

"Yep."

"Do you have a date?"

"I'm going alone."

"OK, but why not get a date? Your mom tells me Suzanne Jones wants you to ask her. I hear she's brilliant, not to mention attractive."

"I don't want to go with Suzanne Jones."

At this point, I could tell Rob's mind was made up. He had a stubborn streak—a Howerton-boy trait, Janice liked to say. There was no way that I was going to make Rob Howerton get a date if he didn't want to. If I insisted, he'd just not go. I knew I would have to convince him that asking Suzanne Jones was in his best interest.

Perhaps if I open my heart to him and share a personal story from my youth . . .

"Rob, when I was a sophomore in high school like you, a friend of a senior named Nancy Mellichamp told me that Nancy would go with me to our annual dance, what we called prom, if I asked her. I couldn't believe it. Nancy Mellichamp was beautiful, a dancer, *and a senior*. But I farted around with indecision, and soon I heard that Nancy had a date with someone else." I paused and took a deep breath. "I've always wondered what that night would have been like if I had asked Nancy and gone to that dance. Years later, I heard she became a flamenco dancer in Madrid."

Rob stayed quiet. He looked pensive. As Janice called us up for dinner, I thought I'd nailed it.

As we finished eating, my wife asked Rob, "Did your dad talk to you about getting a date for prom?"

Rob said, "Yes. Dad thinks I should ask Suzanne Jones so we can have sex."

Janice's jaw dropped. Her eyes widened as she turned her reddening face to me, and without saying a word, I knew she was screaming, "*What in the hell did you say to our son?*"

Rob went to the prom without a date. He had a wonderful time.

Life Lessons
- Fathers don't always know best (and it's OK to go to the prom alone).
- When you want to make sure you have communicated something effectively to someone, ask them to tell you what they think they heard you say so that you can improve your effective communicating skills.

WILL YOU SEE ME NOW?

Two hours into my slumber in the night quarters provided by the administrative watch officer of Portsmouth Naval Hospital, the phone rang. It was the night chief.

"Lieutenant Howerton, you are needed in the ER. Someone here just shot himself."

I wasn't sure that I heard that right. "You mean someone shot himself, and now he's in the ER."

"No, I mean someone shot himself *in* the ER."

I threw on my uniform and raced down to the emergency room. When I got to the other side of the "staff only" double doors, I stopped and took in the scene. A black revolver lay on the terra-cotta floor in front of the nurses' station; security guards were interviewing an orderly; surgery was underway in the trauma room; and a night supervisor was consoling an ER nurse, whose shocked face was as white as her bleached uniform.

The senior security officer came over and briefed me. A young sailor had come into the ER after midnight, complaining of lower back pain. The triage nurse told him he might want to visit a back pain clinic during the week because this was an ER on Saturday night with heart attacks, broken bones, and trauma, and it could be hours before he would be seen.

The seaman said, "I'll be right back," and he left. A few minutes later, he returned and waited patiently at the nurses' station to get the attention of the nurse who'd spoken to him. When he did, he raised his revolver, put the barrel to his shoulder, pulled the trigger, and said, "Will you see me now?"

Life Lessons
- Some people just won't wait.
- Chronic pain can drive some people crazy.

GULF STATION SLEEPOVER

Being a teenager in Disneyland during the Summer of Love was unlike my first visit as a kid. The scenery was no less enchanting, and the rides were still fantastic. But now, there were additional creations to appreciate, especially those my age.

I couldn't get the Beach Boys' "California Girls" out of my mind, nor did I want to. My sisters and I agreed that we had never seen so many beautiful young people anywhere at one time. We begged Mom and Dad to let us stay until closing, which was not part of Dad's plan. He'd wanted to leave early for a state campground, but we kids mounted a campaign of persistent pestering, begging, and bargaining, and Dad's reluctance gave way.

We didn't leave the park until after midnight. By then, even Dad admitted that Tinkerbell's zip-lining from the Matterhorn to Cinderella's Castle to light the fireworks with her magic wand was worth waiting to see.

The departing hordes from Disneyland and the normal Saturday night Los Angeles County traffic clogged the freeways, and after a couple of bumper-to-bumper hours, Dad's state park destination was still hours away. With exhaustion bearing down, we stopped at a Gulf Station to fill up our Buick pulling a borrowed fold-out Apache tent trailer because our trusty J. C. Higgins tent had come back from Europe in shreds two summers earlier.

While we used the facilities, Dad struck up a conversation with the night attendant, and a few minutes later, he told us we would be setting up our trailer tent for the night right there. Over our protests that a gas station was not a campground and it was a neighborhood of unknown safety on a busy city street, Dad assured us that we had everything we needed: bathrooms, food, and an attendant watching over us all night.

It was the first time we'd ever brushed our teeth in a gas station sink. Soon, we settled into our sleeping bags and drifted off to sleep.

◆　◆　◆

An hour later, we woke up to a bus full of teenagers pulling in and noisily disembarking for bathroom breaks and snacks. We later learned they had been to Disneyland all day.

Above the giggles and shouts, we heard one guy ask, "What's that over there?"

Another loud voice answered, "Looks like a tent."

Silhouettes of giant teenagers began to rise on our green canvas walls.

"Must be a demonstration of some kind."

"Let's check it out."

When the zipper on the entrance flap began to rise, my father the preacher sat up, held his size-twelve wingtip over his head, and yelled as loud as I've ever heard him yell, "Get the hell out of here!"

Shrieks erupted outside, followed by pattering soles, chortles, and guffaws. Their bus left soon thereafter.

Our adrenaline kept us up until a few hours before dawn.

Life Lessons

- If you camp at a gas station, don't plan on getting much sleep.
- Never open a closed tent without permission.

THE BEST TEACHER I EVER HAD

My sixth-grade teacher, Mrs. Nicholson, decided to take her other thirty-nine students and me on a bus trip from Blacksburg, Virginia, to Durham and Chapel Hill, North Carolina, and back in a single day. She told us she wanted to expand our horizons by experiencing both the beauty within the Gothic chapel at Duke University and the expansive starry views displayed by the Morehead Planetarium on the University of North Carolina campus. She and her Virginia Tech graduate student husband were to be our only chaperones on this eighteen-hour excursion, a fact that today's helicopter parents might deem impossible.

Our trip went off without a hitch.

How did she pull it off? Her success started in her classroom and on the playground.

Anytime Mrs. Nicholson sensed our attention in class was wandering too far, she detracted us by tossing a beach ball our way and demanded we bat it back to her. Or she might break out in a new song that she would proceed to teach us. With our tension released, Mrs. Nicholson would return to her lesson plan.

At recess, she was a firm believer that the purpose of that period was to expel pent-up kinetic energy stored in our eleven- and twelve-year-old bodies. To ensure participation, she would umpire and referee our games and sometimes join in as a player. When rain or snow kept us inside, she invented sit-down beach ball volleyball with half the class facing the other half at our desks across an imaginary "middle net." Our repetitive twists and arm extensions wore us out, making us capable of sitting still when her teaching began again. Mrs. Nicholson made learning fun.

Acquaintances in neighboring classrooms told us that our random bursting into song was as welcome to their teachers as fingernails scratching a slate blackboard. Mrs. Nicholson ignored them, insisting that she loved our singing, and we loved her for it, even when she taught us show tunes and World War II ditties that would've gagged us before she taught us to like them. Our vocal talents grew, eliciting invitations to sing for civic and garden clubs, retirement homes, hospitals, and our appreciative, disbelieving-their-ears parents. Through rhythm, timing, tone, and harmony, she drilled us on the importance of tight group discipline.

But back to that bus trip. How did she dare take forty students, many of whom (including me) had received many a U for "unsatisfactory conduct" on our report cards in previous years, on a trip with only herself and her husband to keep us in line?

From the start, Mrs. Nicholson demanded that we pay our way. She established a monetary goal, and every morning for months, we passed around a bucket for allowances, unspent lunch money, pop bottle return deposits, compensation for mowed lawns, babysitting earnings, and quite a few begged parental contributions. She made certain that we had a vested interest in our planned adventure.

But perhaps more importantly, a week before our trip, Mrs. Nicholson read off a list of students' names to join her for a "conference" in the coat closet. I heard my name called, and as I made my way to join a group of other strong-willed kids, I wondered what kind of trouble I'd gotten into now.

But after Mrs. Nicholson huddled us around her, she put her hands on her knees and leaned down until her eyes were level with ours. She took turns looking at each of us as she whispered, "I have called each of you here because you are the leaders of our class. And if our trip is going to be successful, I need each of you to promise both me *and each other* that you will do your part. I need you to be aware of things that are happening and take action—appropriate and kind action—if a classmate starts to get out of hand. I can't do this by myself, and I'm counting on each of you. Do I have your commitment?"

We all nodded or said, "Yes, ma'am."

No adult had ever spoken to me like that.

"Good. I am depending on you," she said, and then she added, "On our trip, spread yourselves out among your classmates; don't sit together as a group. Now, promise me that you will keep this conversation just between us."

We nodded again. That was what leaders would do.

Our trip succeeded for many reasons, not the least of which was the commitment we made in that closet. When one of us saw someone getting out of hand, we intervened. To this day, I feel proud that Mrs. Nicholson put her trust in me. It was one of the smartest things that I have ever witnessed a teacher do.

Mrs. Nicholson, wherever you are, I know that I join many of your former students in saying that you were the best teacher I ever had. We are forever grateful.

Life Lessons
- Having a great teacher is a gift that can last a lifetime.
- Sometimes, even the people you least expect to succeed just need an opportunity to rise to the occasion.

THE POWER OF GOALS

Growing up in Blacksburg, I observed that college students could have a lot of fun getting educated. So, when I enrolled at Wake Forest, I set two goals for myself: 1) have a great time, and 2) make good enough grades to get into law school.

How do you think that worked out for me?

If you guessed that I achieved excellence in having fun, you would be correct. I had a blast. Unfortunately, after three years of focusing on that first goal, achieving my second was at risk.

Janice, my soon-to-be fiancée, was a diligent student and a perpetual earner of Dean's List accolades. Unlike me, she was projected to graduate cum laude—with distinction. I started imagining what it would feel like to see those Latin words on her diploma hanging next to my more undistinctive version.

I wondered if I could catch up.

◆　◆　◆

At the college registrar's office, I met a woman whose face conveyed either that she'd already heard of every circumstance, excuse, or illogical request that students could concoct or that she'd inherited tolerance and understanding at birth; I couldn't decide which. She wore a sensible cardigan clipped beneath her chin with a silver chain, letting her sweater lie open, perhaps a preparation should the heat of a conversation rise. A yellow pencil impaled her graying curls. She leaned forward on her elbows, arms crossed, and asked, "What can I help you with?"

"Could you figure out what grades I would have to make my senior year to graduate cum laude?"

Her expression did not change one iota. "Of course. Let me pull your file, and we shall see."

A minute later, she returned to the counter, opened a manila folder, took the yellow pencil out of her hair, and started punching the keys of an adding machine with the pencil's pink eraser. When she finished her calculations, she looked up at me and said, "Well, it's possible, but you'll have to make all As. Well, that's not exactly right. You could make one B."

When I left the registrar's office, hopelessness set in. I had never come close to a 4.0 grade point average any semester. Then my mind kept picturing those dueling diplomas, and I decided it was time to reset my goals. This time I only had one: make all As my senior year.

And I did.

And Janice has never forgiven me.

Life Lessons
- Never underestimate the power of setting personal goals.
- Some goals are more important than others.

DIDN'T YOU SEE ME?

One autumn, after visiting our middle son, Drew, at the University of Southern California, Janice and I decided to visit Big Sur. In a rented red Mustang convertible, we headed north on the beautiful Pacific Coast Highway.

In the late afternoon, as we approached the outskirts of our first destination, Cambria, the weather was perfect. Our top was down, the radio blasting solid gold tunes, and I took it slow and easy, soaking in every moment of this special journey. I was not concerned when I got close enough to realize that we were following a California Highway Patrol car in the distance. I'd set my cruise control on sixty, a conservative five miles over the speed limit. But as I closed the distance between us, the patrol car's brakes lit up, and it swerved off onto the highway's gravel shoulder. As soon as we passed, in the rearview mirror, I saw the patrol car twirling its blue lights and spewing gravel in long trails until its tires gripped highway asphalt. It roared up to our bumper.

"Oh, shit," I said as I put on my turn signal and pulled over.

Janice, looking youthful and stunning in her sunglasses, said something like, "It's OK. Don't worry. You weren't speeding, were you?"

A tall officer of the law marched up to my door and boomed, "License and registration!" His face was red, his jaw muscles jumping with each clench of his teeth.

I gave the officer what he asked for and he stomped off.

He was just as mad when he came back. As he handed me my documents, he said, "Didn't you see me in front of you? You were doing sixty in a forty-five zone behind a highway patrol car!" These words came to me with an intonation that suggested, "Are you a blind man? What kind of complete idiot are you, keeping me from getting home on time on a Friday afternoon?"

A forty-five zone? Uh-oh. I took a deep breath and started talking. "Officer, I admit I had my cruise control on sixty because I thought the speed limit was fifty-five like it's been for miles and miles. I must have missed the sign. We are in no hurry. We were just going to Cambria, cruising on this beautiful day, celebrating our twenty-fifth wedding anniversary." In truth, our anniversary was back in June, but we'd been calling this our celebratory trip.

The officer stopped writing on his pad and looked at me. Then he extended his neck and lowered his aviator sunglasses to get a better view of Janice, who looked at least fifteen years younger than me versus the fifteen days that she was.

"Ma'am, have you really been married to this man for twenty-five years?" My mind heard, "That's incredible! You look too young and beautiful to be married for twenty-five years to such an imbecile as this dumbass, the lucky stiff."

"Yes, officer," she said with a smile. "We plan to see Hearst Castle and drive up to Big Sur for the first time."

The officer snapped his pad shut. He looked right at me and said, "Sir, you need to pay better attention."

I nodded with vigor.

"You are in California now, and we can get you frontways, backways, and sideways."

"Yes, of course, officer," I said.

Then he looked at Janice and said, "You have a happy anniversary, ma'am."

Life Lessons

- Never speed behind a cop who's on the way home after a long workday.
- Some days, you just get lucky.

A YOKE OF JUSTICE

True confession: I went egging as a teenager.
I learned this prank from a cousin (now a lawyer) and his friend in Mount Airy, North Carolina, while visiting my grandmother Ora. At the time, we might have blamed our delinquency on a roadside market that tempted us by selling four dozen eggs in a paper grocery bag for one dollar. My cousin's friend (also now a lawyer) had a convertible Willys Jeepster, a perfect mobile platform to launch a barrage of shells on an undeserving something or someone. It seemed funny at the time.

As we loaded the last bag of eggs into the Jeepster, the bag broke, and four dozen eggs splattered onto Ora's cement driveway. The mass of yolks and whites began flowing down toward grandmother's garage. Quick thinking by one of the future barristers led to our hosing the mass down into a convenient drain. But an eggy yellow and its accompanying stench remained.

One of our underdeveloped minds convinced the others that fire would kill the odor. Gasoline and a match soon merged in a whooshing conflagration of flames that also began to creep toward the garage. The garden hose saved us again. Fireworks were our explanation for the sofa-sized smoky smudge on Grandmother's clean cement.

Despite my Mount Airy experience, I became an ambassador for the migration of this bad practice to my hometown. In subsequent months, egging proliferated into sectional warfare among the boys of Blacksburg.

◆ ◆ ◆

One night, I was driving my mother's Buick Electra 225 with a carload of pals seeking egging revenge. We found our targets, and late into the foray, I grew increasingly frustrated that as the driver, I never got to throw an egg at our antagonists.

"Give me an egg!" I demanded. My friends dropped one in my right hand as I gripped the steering wheel with my left. I wound up for a side-armed hurl and launched that egg with all my might.

Splat, the eggshell and yolk sounded against the glass of my rolled-up window.

The car fell silent as all occupants sucked in oxygen for the gales of chortles and shrieks that followed. I hung my head and watched that scrambled mess flow down the upholstered door, upon which the yellow tracks never came out. An errant custard milkshake was my explanation, which my parents seemed to doubt.

I never went egging again.

Life Lessons
- Never light gasoline on a hill.
- If you really need to throw something out your car window, roll down the window first.

FIGHTING TO CARE

One afternoon, I was at my desk looking out at the black-and-white Holstein dairy cows in the field next to Granville Hospital when my executive assistant came in and informed me that someone needed to speak to me about the care of her grandfather, an inpatient two floors above. As CEO of my first hospital, I'd been trying to teach (some would say preach) that it was a privilege to serve patients and we should fight for every precious opportunity to do so, and if complaints about service arose, then we should view them as an opportunity to improve.

"Send her in," I said without hesitation.

I stood up and walked to the doorway, where my assistant introduced me to a young woman, thirty-something, wearing a floral print dress. We shook hands, and I offered her one of the two armchairs in front of my desk. I sat in the other chair and positioned a legal pad on my crossed leg to take notes on whatever had occurred. I asked her how I could help.

"I don't want to get nobody in trouble. We love the people caring for PawPaw. That's what I call my granddaddy."

"Please, tell me what happened."

"I saw . . . are you sure they won't get in too much trouble? I wouldn't want that."

Not knowing where this complaint was headed, I wasn't ready to commit. I smiled and asked, "You say you saw . . . what exactly?"

"I saw . . . well, first, they got into an argument about who was supposed to feed PawPaw. Things got . . . well, they got out of hand."

"Out of hand? In what way?"

"They got to throwing food at each other . . . across PawPaw's bed."

"They did what?" My voice was louder than I'd intended.

"It started with a yeast roll. Your cafeteria makes the best rolls. She threw one at him. Then he threw a piece of broccoli back at her. Then the mashed potatoes and iced tea. They kind of had a food fight."

I tried not to think of my two college friends. "That's terrible!"

"Wait, now. Hear me out. They didn't get nothing on him. Or me. I was sitting in the corner."

I couldn't see how this mattered. Unbelievable! I should fire them both on the spot.

"You see," she went on, "they were actually fighting over who got to care for PawPaw. It's kind of sweet when you think about it."

Sweet? I felt my eyes widen as if their new aperture might suction wisdom out of the ether. I took a deep breath and said, "I am so, so sorry. Please accept our sincerest apology. Please, would you help me make sure I have these circumstances straight? Our staff threw the food that one of them was supposed to feed your grandfather at each other over your grandfather's bed? Because . . . they both wanted to feed him?"

"Yes. That's right. But he's not eating much these days. He's at the end of his time on this earth. He never even knew it happened. Slept through the whole thing. Then those two said they were sorry and cleaned it all up. One of them brought in another tray. But PawPaw didn't wake up."

After taking notes and offering profuse apologies, I promised appropriate discipline for the two involved. I knew I had to do something, and quick. This kind of story had legs. I was probably the last one in the hospital to know about it already. (Later that afternoon, the principals involved confirmed the granddaughter's accuracy with apt remorse.)

As the woman made her way out of my office, she stopped in the doorway. She turned her smile toward me and looked at me with warm brown eyes. Then she said, "I know you got to do something. People will be waiting to see what you do. But if I were you, I'd figure a way to keep those two. Maybe you could suspend them or something temporary. Then, I'd welcome them back if I were you. Those two really care about their patients. We need more people like them."

And that's exactly what I did.

Life Lessons
- Caring for people is worth fighting for—figuratively speaking.
- Judgment is best with a compassionate eye toward those who care.

WORDS CAN HAVE MULTIPLE MEANINGS

As a sophomore in my algebra II class at Blacksburg High, I had the best seat in the class—right behind Janis Perdue, the gorgeous junior cheerleader. I had the biggest crush on her, and to be sitting right behind her the entire year had to be a gift from heaven. She could have her pick of the handsome and athletic upperclassmen while she wasn't dating Virginia Tech football players. To say that she was out of my league would be like saying the universe is big. But there I sat, every morning, two feet behind her, staring at her luscious brown hair in its pageboy haircut, inhaling whatever perfume she was intoxicating me with that day. And to think, earlier that fall, she walked in and picked the desk in front of me, a seat she would keep for the entire year.

At first, we didn't say more than hello to each other. Her attention was on her friends in front of and beside her. Every now and then, she might ask me what our teacher said or check an assignment. I may have helped her with an equation a couple of times. She was not as interested in math as I was. I dreamed that someday she might ask me to tutor her, but that was as likely as the Beatles requesting to play at one of our sock hops.

As the year went on, we had enough polite conversations to make me comfortable to share with her that her sweater, a cream cable knit V-neck, had a loop of yarn pulled out on her shoulder that I knew she couldn't see. I'd learned from my mother and sisters that if it weren't fixed, then it could expand and ruin her beautiful sweater, so I decided to be helpful and tell her about it. But instead of calling it a pulled loop of yarn or a snag, I used the specific word that my mother and sister had taught me to describe an errant strand of wool on a sweater, possibly nicked by a sharp object, that could be repaired by using a needle to redirect it back under the weave where it belonged. I felt certain that Janis would appreciate my telling her, perhaps even thank me for it, and that somehow my observation and knowledge of what needed repair might lead to our becoming good friends.

That was how it came to be that I initiated the first conversation with my crush of that year, the one and only Janis Perdue, by leaning forward and whispering, "Janis, you have a prick on your shoulder."

She laughed so hard that our teacher almost threw her out of class. I never learned which of the multiple meanings of what I said made her laugh the most.

Our conversations became less frequent after that. We never became good friends.

Life Lessons
- Your mother and sister's use of a word doesn't necessarily make it safe for public use.
- Good intentions do not always overcome everything you say.

DAD'S ILLNESS: PART IV

"Your mother is on line one."

Lost in the paperwork covering my desk, I looked up to see my executive assistant's head peeking around my door that I hadn't heard her open. There was a pained smile on her face.

Before I could ask what was wrong, she added, "She sounds upset." Then she closed the door to my office at Alamance County Hospital and gave me privacy.

That Mom seemed upset was unusual. Her phone calls were usually all business, dispensing with emotional greetings or how-are-you small talk and getting right to the point. Most often, her first word was "Listen."

I pressed the flashing light on my desk phone and said, "Hello, Mom."

"Richard. Dick is sick. I need you to come. Now."

From her tone, I knew at once that depression had my father in its grip again.

◆ ◆ ◆

The hour-and-twenty-minute drive from Burlington to Mount Airy gave me time to reflect on my three previous experiences with Dad's recurring illness: first, as a naive second grader; second, as a high school senior who denied the profound impact my father's depression had on me; and the last time, when I, upon hearing the news, went crazy mowing the backyard until I was graced with an epiphany of understanding.

This time, Dad's illness surprised me more than ever. I'd hoped that retirement would bring Dad stress-free peace and tranquility and that his depression might retire too. Despite it all, I felt confident that I could help Mom with Dad. But nothing prepared me for what I was about to see.

After parking in their driveway, I bounded up the steps to the front porch and entered without knocking. I strode through the foyer and into the den. There, I saw Dad sitting on the ottoman of my favorite chair, a swivel rocker upholstered in a fabric that depicted red-coated huntsmen, hounds, and foxes. Dad sat motionless, bent over his extended arms, his two hands holding the open end of one sock in midair. He held his bent right knee up near his chest, bare toes pointing toward the ceiling. His eyes were fixed and staring at his suspended foot.

"Dad," I said, thinking, *What in the hell is going on?*

My father stayed frozen in place.

"Dad!" I said louder this time.

Still no response.

Mom was standing in the doorway to the kitchen, her arms raising open palms toward me as if she was ready for whatever I planned to do.

"How long has he been like this?"

Mom couldn't say.

I knelt and got close to my father's face. I hoped my

words expressed caring and firm reassurance as I tried to move his limbs. But his body's muscles remained locked, holding him in horrifying stillness. I kept calling his name, trying to reach him, as I pressed down on his arms and leg, worrying that my actions might hurt him, pull a muscle, even snap a tendon or, God forbid, a bone. Slowly, I struggled to inch his leg to the floor and his arms back into his lap. When he was sitting almost upright, I pulled his socks over the cold skin of his white-blue feet and put on and tied his favorite brown wingtip shoes.

Dad stirred. He looked at me with red, watery eyes. His face had the look of a child, and I wondered if I looked like that when he visited my bedside when I had the measles and felt lost in the doom of Khrushchev's "We will bury you!"

After Mom and I got Dad to his feet, we led him to my car. My hand helped lower his head so it wouldn't bump the doorframe. I buckled his seat belt, and we began our journey to the caring therapists at North Carolina Baptist Hospital in Winston-Salem for what would be his last hospitalization for depression.

Life Lessons
- Nothing prepares you to see a loved one in the grips of a mental illness.
- Depression can be a lifelong companion.

YOUR SON IS FINE, BUT . . .

One lazy afternoon from our row of beach chairs on Atlantic Beach, North Carolina, Janice and I watched over our three-year-old son Seth playing in ankle-deep foam.

Suddenly Seth shrieked and ran toward us, holding up a blood-spewing finger. We leaped up, wrapped Seth in a towel, bolted to our car, and drove straight to the ER of Carteret General Hospital, where the staff took him back to the trauma room for immediate treatment.

As I was a hospital administrator familiar with the workings and protocols of ERs, Janice suggested that I go back with Seth, whose persistent wails evoked superlatives from the staff. To the ER physician and his assistant, I confessed that I had no idea what had caused Seth's injury—it could have been a crab, a bluefish, a piece of glass. But for some reason, as I watched the doctor take the first of a dozen stitches in Seth's fingertip, I felt compelled to announce to the caregivers that I was a hospital administrator in Burlington.

Twenty minutes later, the ER nurse delivered a stitched-up Seth to Janice in the waiting room. And then she rolled me out in a wheelchair, as was the custom for someone who had passed out.

To Janice, she said, "Your son's going to be fine. But I don't know about this here *hospital administrator!*"

Life Lessons
- Pride goes before the fall.
- Parenting can be hazardous to your health.

GAME FILM

Though I played on Blacksburg High School's football teams for four years, I only started my senior year. As an offensive tackle, I was anonymous to every fan in the stands except my parents and girlfriend. The only time the announcer mentioned my name was during pregame introductions, when most people were busy finding a seat, buying hotdogs or popcorn, and chatting with friends.

During a game, the only time the announcer called my name was for a fumble recovery. When Billy Smith, our fine quarterback and my good friend, got hit in the backfield, I saw the game ball, a brown Wilson football with white stripes on each end, lying on the green grass. I fell on it. My parents and girlfriend praised my accomplishment after the game. Even a few teammates patted me on the back. I felt proud that I recovered that football even though we lost the game.

But it wasn't the whole story. And I knew it.

The real story was that I was playing across the line against someone whom I feared. He was a mean giant of a man from Narrows High School. He wasn't any bigger than a couple of guys that I practiced against, but something about him that I still don't understand made me hold back against him—the worst thing I could have done. I got to recover that fumble because I had missed that guy completely with such a pathetic attempt of an arm block that he stormed like a freight train loaded with Narrows coal and creamed Billy. The ball popped loose and landed in the grass right in front of me. I leaped and clutched the ball in a tight fetal position as I'd been coached to do. After the referee whistled the play dead, I heard the announcer say, "Fumble recovered by Howerton." The crowd cheered.

I decided to keep my mouth shut about that play. Even if I did miss my block, at least I recovered the ball, right? What good would it do?

The weekend passed, and on Monday, our team looked at the black-and-white game film before we practiced. I started to sweat, wondering if those fuzzy images on the screen would rat me out. When that fumble play lit the screen, our head coach said, "Nice fumble recovery, Richard." I could breathe again.

Then the coach reversed the projector so he could see my nice play again, I assumed. But this time he said, "Wait a minute! Wait a damn minute. What was that?"

What that was was my pathetic arm thrown out to block my Narrows man, who swept it aside like he would a limp weeping willow branch and stormed in practically untouched to slaughter my teammate.

My head coach and the whole team watched that play three more times. Then, my coach glared at me with his piercing blue eyes until I said, "I missed my man," and hung my head in shame.

Life Lessons

- An opponent should be respected, studied, anticipated, and prepared for, but fear can kill your ability to perform at your best.
- Admitting your past mistakes is the best first step toward improvement in the future.

HAIRCUT SURPRISE

Two days before Janice and I were married, I learned that Duke University had accepted me as a graduate student pursuing a master's degree in health administration. Janice's teaching job provided our room and board, but to pay for my first-semester tuition, I had to sell my car.

With the bill for the second semester on the horizon, I searched for alternative financing that led me to apply for a scholarship with the navy, which I was glad to receive. After a physical and swearing-in, I became an ensign in the Medical Service Corps of the US Naval Reserve. My first order was to report to the commanding officer of the NROTC unit at Duke.

Within an hour, I sat across the desk from a captain in the "regular" navy, who received me with congratulations and paternal tolerance. He told me that my only duty as an officer in his command was to be a good student and pick up my paycheck every two weeks. Then he added, "To get your paycheck, you will need to cut your hair."

That was a surprise. I wasn't supposed to wear a uniform, nor was I to acquire one until I graduated, so why would I need to cut my hair? The captain cut off my mental debate by instructing me to go to the campus barber, get a military regulation haircut, return to him, and have my photo taken for my official ID card, and then I would be on my way.

When I told the barber that I needed a military haircut, he was a little too eager to attack my shoulder-length hair that I had styled for my wedding in a cool custom shag. That barber pruned me with a speed that made my eyes water. Back at the NROTC office, the captain smiled, praised the results of my follicular assault, and declared it a success. I didn't recognize myself on my photo ID.

Outside, Duke's gray Gothic campus did nothing to lift my plunging mood, especially when I remembered that I'd locked my keys in the apartment that morning. I had to mope around until Janice got home from school. Since my bicycle had been stolen the week before, it was a long, hot walk back to our apartment. When I saw Janice's car in the parking lot, my spirits soared. A hug from Janice is what I needed to restore my sulking soul. I ran up the stairs and knocked on our apartment door.

Janice opened the door, took one look at me, screamed, and slammed the door in my face.

Life Lessons
- Don't surprise your new bride with a shockingly bad haircut.
- Graduating from graduate school debt-free is worth a bad haircut.

LIVING IN A PARSONAGE

Early one Saturday morning, Mom and I were at her kitchen table drinking coffee. After Dad died, I tried to visit her in Mount Airy as often as possible, and those times were precious. Our conversations were never loquacious. She might mention the Sunday school lesson she was "working up," pausing to point out a cardinal or chickadee in her bird feeder. We traded a few words about family happenings.

I decided to share that someone I knew had done something that I found shocking, and I asked her what she thought about it.

Mom looked at me and said, "Richard, after living in a parsonage, there's nothing human beings do that shocks me."

Life Lessons
- A preacher's wife knows things that would shock you.
- Wisdom grows with age.

NICE, NICE, VERY NICE

When my brother-in-law, Damon, graduated from college, I suggested that he accompany me on an upcoming business trip to New York City as a graduation gift. I figured he could tour the Big Apple for the first time while I attended my seminar.

We arrived on a Sunday morning, and I enjoyed witnessing Damon's exposure to the sights and sounds of Manhattan circa 1983. We walked Times Square, Fifth Avenue, and Central Park before taking the subway to Greenwich Village. After visiting Washington Square, we entered the Knickerbocker and ordered drinks from a table near the bar. Amid the patrons enjoying late afternoon libations, Damon looked as if this first day of his trip had exceeded his expectations, so much so that he raised his glass and said, "This has been nice, nice! *Very nice!*"

Proud that my travel mentoring was appreciated, I echoed Damon's toast in loud agreement, saying, "Nice, nice! *Very* nice."

Just when I made my return toast, a woman wearing a short tennis dress exited right next to our table. The tall, tennis-racket-wielding man following her wheeled around, glared at me, and shouted, "That's my *wife* you're talking about!" I watched him turn a deeper red as he boomed, "People like you make me hate this place. You asshole!" He drew back his racket as if he were about to launch a forehand swing to my face.

His brutish outburst shocked me into a silence that overtook the entire bar and restaurant. In the quiet, my mind raced. What was he talking about? My toast? "Nice, nice, very nice"? Oh, shit—he thought I was praising his wife's posterior as it passed by our table.

I had to say something.

Perhaps it was Janice's little brother's presence. Or maybe it was the metal tennis racket waggling at eye level that helped me say, "I'm *so* sorry, sir. I was talking to my brother-in-law about his first day ever in New York City. We'd just seen the sights, and I was agreeing with him that it had been a 'nice, nice, very nice' *day*. I was talking about our *day*."

The look on his face didn't change. For an instant I feared that I had insulted this jerk's wife by declaring her behind was unworthy of my notice.

Then the husband's posture began to shift. His shoulders eased down, and he lowered his weapon. "Well," he said, still staring at me. "Be careful. What you say could get you killed in New York City." And then he turned and left.

Life Lessons
- What is overheard can be misinterpreted.
- It's often better to defuse a misunderstanding with an apology, even if you don't owe one.

THE ELIZABETH RIVER

The phone ringing beside me roused me from a deep sleep. When I managed to get the receiver to my ear, I heard a voice say, "One of our patients is in the river." I hoped I was dreaming. I wasn't. To me, as the administrative watch officer of Portsmouth Naval Hospital for the night, that news was bad enough. But it got worse.

As I yanked on my lieutenant uniform, my mind ticked through what the night chief had relayed to me: a patient had escaped from the psych ward, jumped into the Elizabeth River, and started swimming toward Norfolk, and two hospital corpsmen had followed him into the river, where they now remained.

Approaching Hospital Point, my stomach clenched at the sight of the flashing lights of a single security vehicle near the water. When I arrived, the security petty officer updated me in short bursts: "Patient suicidal. Broke out. Corpsman gave chase into the river. Another corpsman in pursuit. Called it in. They're about eighty yards out. Treading deep water. No splashes, no struggles. Hear voices, now and then. Quiet voices, no panic. No boat to send out.

Water's cold. Hypothermia risk. Naval Shipyard called. Tug on the way. No known ETA."

I thanked him and asked that he move his vehicle so that its headlights pointed out toward where the patient and corpsmen were in the water. He did as I ordered, but when the headlights scanned across the water, I saw nothing but black ripples and reflections of the lights of the Norfolk waterfront in the distance.

Then I asked if the Portsmouth or Norfolk police had been called. I recalled having seen their boats in the river and helicopters overhead.

"Civilians, sir?" he asked.

"Yes. We need all the help we can get," I said, which sent him off speaking into his walkie-talkie that answered him in short squawks.

The medical watch officer arrived. He was a plastic surgeon commander, and he asked whether I thought it was time to inform our commanding officer, a tough, no-nonsense rear admiral. Though this medical officer outranked me, I knew from previous night watch duty with him that he drew a distinct line between medical and administrative matters. Until a patient was treatable, he would see this situation as my responsibility. I told him if he didn't call the CO, I would. He went off to do so.

◆ ◆ ◆

Though more hospital staff gathered on the scene around me, I saw nothing in the water but what my imagination assumed might be an occasional head bobbing in the distance. I felt alone. Faint, undiscernible voices reached my ears a couple of times. They still didn't sound like fighting voices. That was good. But the voices weren't getting closer and that was bad. But worse, there were no sounds of a rescue boat approaching.

The security guard with the radio came back and told me that the night chief had called the civilian police as I requested and the Norfolk Naval Station to see if a helicopter was available. I nodded at the chief's good initiative.

By now, the three men had been in the water for over twenty minutes. My body shivered with certainty that cold water and exhaustion were taking their toll. They could only tread water for so long. I could lose all three.

Just then, another corpsman approached me. He said he was a champion swimmer from Florida and a trained lifesaver, and he volunteered to swim out and help. The young man seemed strong, and his words bore the ring of truth. My mind dissected my options. Wait for the boat? How long would they last? Try to save them now? Put another swimmer in that dark water? Risk losing another man?

My gut answered. "Go, but don't set any records on the way out. You'll need all your energy when you get there."

From an ambulance that had arrived, someone suggested giving the volunteer lifesaver a wooden bodyboard as a kickboard float, and I agreed. As the third man splashed into the blackness, I swallowed back vomit, fearing I'd made the wrong decision, sending another into harm's way.

More time passed. Five minutes? Ten minutes? Our commanding officer arrived along with the shipyard tugboat and civilian police helicopter. A navy helicopter joined in. Dueling spotlights searched the waters at the end of the headlight beams.

What was happening? Everyone wanted to know.

Then word came. The tug crew had pulled three men out alive, all corpsmen. The Florida swim champion had arrived just in time to keep one of the first corpsmen from drowning.

The patient was lost beneath the dark water. Several days later, his body was found downriver, miles away.

◆   ◆   ◆

After dawn, there were briefings and notifications to be made up the chain of command and reports to be filed. It took me most of the day to write my official statement. The press was all over the incident, having monitored their police scanners. Weeks later, a power boat was appropriated for our hospital to have on-site for emergencies.

I have second-guessed my actions on that night a thousand times, and again writing about this now. I was lucky that there was only one death that night. I was lucky that the young lifesaver was who and what he said he was. I was lucky someone suggested that a bodyboard could be a kickboard float. I wish I'd called the local fire departments; perhaps their ladders, spotlights, hoses, ropes, and maybe even a rescue craft would have made a difference. I wish I had done something that saved the patient's life.

I have always wondered what the best decision would have been. And I always will.

Life Lessons
- When you're in charge, it's possible to feel alone even if surrounded by a throng of people. Act anyway.
- Sometimes, you'll always wonder if you did the right thing.

AIRPORT BOOT

As I approached my sixth decade, my left Achilles tendon morphed into an old rubber band, which led to its prescribed six-week cohabitation with an inflatable, plastic orthopedic boot. Complete with fashionable Velcro straps, it came with a hand pump that looked like a miniature football, with two metal prongs attached to the ends for inflation or deflation as the need arose. Packing for a business trip to Las Vegas, I decided to keep the pump handy should I be asked to remove my boot by Atlanta's TSA inspectors, but they paid me no special mind.

Following the conference, I approached the Vegas airport security with the same boot strategy. After a scan in the stand-up-hold-your-hands-over-your-head X-ray booth, a TSA agent directed me over to a man wearing a blue blazer. "Please sit down, Mr. Howerton," he said.

I did so, thinking he would ask me to remove my boot, but his serious half-smile made me wait for further instructions.

From the shadows of my peripheral vision, I became aware of movement, as if shadows were closing in on me. Out of the dimly lit background, shadowy figures emerged.

Some held automatic weapons. At a practiced distance, they stopped in silence. An eerie quiet smothered the previous cacophony.

"Mr. Howerton," the blue-blazer man asked in a calm, firm voice, "what do you have in your right front pants pocket?"

Why was he asking me that? I just went through the body scanner. Didn't he just need to check my boot? Oh, my right front pocket—that's where my hand pump is. That was it. I'll show him.

Reaching into that pocket, I said, "Oh, this is what I—"

I caught myself.

I was about to say, "Blow up my boot with."

Lord, have mercy. I almost told this trigger-happy SWAT team, "This is what I blow up my boot with."

With the tips of my fingers halted at the rim of my pocket, I started over. "Officer, the hand pump I use to *inflate and deflate* my orthopedic boot is in this pocket." He nodded for me to continue. I pulled the hand pump out slowly and offered it to him.

The blue-blazer man must have given some secret signal because the shadowy figures evaporated. The sounds of luggage slapping conveyors and rote TSA instructions returned.

The blue-blazer man shook his head. Then he leaned over, looked me in the eye, and said, "Mr. Howerton, don't *ever* put that pump in your pocket again going through airport security. It looks like a remote bomb detonator. Now, you have a nice day."

Life Lessons
- Empty your pockets of everything before being scanned at the airport.
- Think before you speak. It might even save your life.

ORA AND THE SNAKE

One afternoon, as Grandmother Ora watched me and my sisters romp in her swimming pool, my older sister, Carol, came over to me with a worried look. "There's something in the drainage ledge over there," she said.

My grandmother's pool was a cement pond, a concrete rectangle fed by mountain creek water through subterranean pipes. The pool's green water rose until it overflowed into a concrete trough along the interior wall, from which it drained through holes and pipes in an adjacent field. There was no filtration system, and you couldn't see beyond three feet into its depths.

"Oh, don't be such a scaredy-cat. It's probably just a frog," I said. We often played with baby frogs, naming them when we gave them rides on inflatable rafts.

"No, it's not," Carol insisted. "It's something else!"

After further heckling, I said, "Show me," and we sloshed through waist-deep water to take a closer look. She was right; what I saw was too big and too black and too long to be a frog. It had to be a snake.

"A snake! A snake!" we screamed, racing up the ladder and running to our grandmother's chair, where we bounced around, pointing and shouting about the lurking monster in her pool.

Grandmother Ora shook her head and told us to hush. She was a Low Gap, North Carolina, girl. Growing up in that village notched into the side of the Blue Ridge Mountains, she was used to all manners of creatures. My grandmother set aside the bowl of half-runners that she was snapping, rose from her favorite metal bouncy chair, and headed to her garage, from which she emerged toting a simple garden hoe, though I knew she could have chosen her garden pick or ax.

My seventy-five-year-old grandmother moseyed around the pool until she reached the spot where we'd spied the serpent in the gutter. She stood on the wall, lowered the metal end of the hoe, and poked the beast. The snake sprang to life, wrapping itself around the right angle of the hoe blade until it became a slithering ball.

Then my calm grandmother swung the wooden handle up, lifting that writhing serpentine mass over her head for a split second before she slammed it down onto the concrete with a ferocious thud. Without pause, she repeated her pummeling until a lifeless length of black scales fell to the concrete. With a final whack, she separated the snake's triangular head from its thick body. Then she bent over and picked up the bleeding body by its tail, stood up, whipped it around her head, and let it fly into her chicken coop forty feet away. With her trusty hoe, she scooped up the snake's head with its curved venomous fangs locked open in its white cottonmouth, strolled over to her flower garden, and buried it among her purple irises.

My sisters and I stood gaping in silent shock as Grandmother Ora returned to her favorite chair. She returned her bowl of half-runners to her lap, started snapping them, and said, "What are y'all looking at? Haven't you ever seen a water moccasin before?"

Life Lessons
- A garden hoe can be a lethal weapon.
- Never underestimate a grandmother.

EDUCATIONAL MISADVICE

As a twenty-nine-year-old hospital CEO, I embraced the axiom that we should be "forever learners." It made perfect sense to me that if one hopes to "stay current" in one's profession, one must perpetually seek new education. Too, I saw imparting this wisdom has a purposeful calling and an obligation to my profession as a healthcare executive. I was proud when my espousing this educational righteousness had any part in leading an associate to seek new knowledge, new certification, an advanced degree, or a new skill.

One day, I decided to encourage my executive assistant, whom I'd inherited from my predecessor, to think about completing her baccalaureate degree that she'd begun years ago. I meant my encouragement as a compliment and a forthright statement of my belief in her abilities.

She didn't take it that way. The next week, she submitted her resignation.

I was shocked.

Over the next several days, I pleaded with her to reconsider. I swore that I meant what I said to her was an expression of my faith in her, not a personal criticism of her current capabilities. I assured her that I felt extraordinarily fortunate to work with her. I confessed how much I needed her and depended on her excellent work and her knowledge of the community and medical politics history. I begged her to stay, insisting that I would be lost without her.

She was unmoved. Nothing I said convinced her that her first impression was incorrect—my encouraging her to return to complete her college education meant that I was not happy with her current level of performance, I wanted her to leave, and her going back to school full-time would be my best means to accomplish her departure.

On the last day we worked together, she told me through tears that becoming the hospital CEO's executive assistant had been the goal of her entire career. As she walked out the door, she said, "This was my dream job. I hope you find someone better."

I felt like a total shit jerk. I still do.

Life Lessons
- Before giving unsolicited career advice, first ask about that person's dreams.
- If you miscommunicate, try your best to set it right.

BIBLE CONVENTION

Attendance at the Southern Baptist Convention helped my father finance two of our family's cross-country camping trips. My father and mother serving as "messengers," official church representatives, came with travel allowances and tax deductions. Babysitters were expensive, so my parents took us along to many of the sessions, thinking that, perhaps, we might be inspired or learn something by the holy experience.

Attending these conventions as an eight-year-old was like sitting through a long church service with an interminably boring business meeting immediately after with no time for snacks in between. Despite occasional snacks, there wasn't much to feed a developing soul. But when I turned eleven and an agenda item about Bible translations was introduced, my boredom ceased.

Then, I witnessed grownups, mostly men in their Sunday finest, get up and either endorse or protest the proper translation to be included in the next published Holy Bible by Broadman Press, the denomination's publisher.

The crowd countered with groans of disgust or shouts of approval. Amid boos and cheers, words like "eternal salvation" or "eternal damnation" and "God's will" and "You're Satan's messenger!" echoed to the rafters.

The heat of discontent slicked blows, strained neck cords, and flushed faces. Whenever I saw people this mad in the movies, fisticuffs followed, or mobs formed, and someone got hurt. If one of these messengers carried a gun, someone could get shot. And to think, all this ruckus was over which words should be printed as Holy Scripture.

Before things escalated, someone called the question, and a vote was taken. That one side was declared the winner did nothing to convince me that consensus was reached. Forgiveness was not in the air.

In the years that followed, I've learned that the Bible many of us use today was largely formed through selections by various individuals, councils, and synods about three hundred years after the death of Jesus Christ. Imagining myself transported back into the midst of those deliberations, I wonder how many discussions, arguments, damnations, and threats may have occurred in those ancient gatherings before final decisions were made. At some point during those imaginary journeys, I find myself back at that Southern Baptist Convention, watching those messengers voice their absolute certainties that they and they alone were articulating the correct will of God.

Our Holy Scripture could result from votes at past Bible conventions or from the sheer will of a group or individual in power, divinely inspired. Perhaps, or perhaps not.

Life Lessons

- Don't underestimate what people will do when they think God is on their side.
- Bible conventions can be scary places.

FRIDAY NIGHT VOICES

One beautiful Friday evening in September, Janice and I planned an at-home date night. With our two young sons in bed, we settled in to enjoy a dinner by candlelight, with windows raised to welcome the near-perfect autumn air—no humidity, comfortably warm with a hint of chill, a harbinger of winter to come. From the high school football stadium one street over, we could hear a pregame soundtrack from a marching band and a public address announcer welcoming the crowd.

When we were about to sit down at our dining room table, we heard three-year-old Seth scream like a banshee. Before we could dash to his bedside, Seth came running down the hall and shrieking with his face bearing a look of sheer terror.

"Oh, Seth! What is it? What's the matter?" Janice asked, kneeling down and hugging his shaking body.

Seth shouted, "God's outside my window! And he's talking to *me!*"

Life Lessons

- Some people think God speaks directly to them. They aren't always correct.
- Advance communication can prevent misunderstandings.

BUSINESS WITH PEOPLE YOU KNOW

In 1996, throughout my two-week trip to Shanghai with representatives from Appalachian State University on a mission to establish a relationship with Fudan University, we attended classes at the business school of Fudan. Here, we learned about China's burgeoning economic development.

One assumption that accompanied me on this trip was that the world's most populous country would be the world's most impersonal place to do business because teeming masses of humanity would make market encounters mere transactions, with little or no time for personal relationships.

One morning in class, I asked a professor if my assumption was true.

"Oh, no," he answered with a smile. "The opposite is true."

"How so?" I asked, wondering if he misunderstood my question.

The professor answered, "China has so many people that we would never do serious business with people we do not know."

Life Lessons
- As the size of a community of human beings grows, so grows its need for personal connections.
- Without the necessary context, even logical conclusions can be incorrect.

MY LITTLE SISTER'S BIG FAITH

One night, Mom, Sarah Jane, and I gathered in our kitchen for supper. Carol, my older sister, was away at college, and Dad was out ministering somewhere. The table around which we sat was one of my father's functional furniture creations. This one he had produced by gluing to plywood a sheet of turquoise Formica imprinted with overlapping multicolored boomerangs, then rimming it with an aluminum edge anchored by counter-sunk screws and attaching it to the top of an old metal dinette table. From his workshop came many such necessary woodworks, ranging from simple cutting boards to tables to chests of drawers and up to bedroom suites of antique reproductions in walnut and cherry.

For some reason, on this night, my little sister felt moved to share her religious beliefs. For several minutes over her plate of Sloppy Joes, she expressed her contemplations with all the fervor and sincerity that her thirteen-year-old soul could convey.

In true big brother form, I found my little sister's confessions to be tedious, juvenile, immature, shallow, and silly compared to the wisdom I'd amassed by living three years longer than she.

"You are *way too young* to know what you believe," I said to Sarah Jane. Then I added, "How much *could* you know?" My words froze my little sister. Several long seconds passed before she thawed enough to burst into tears.

Mom gave me a look that I took to mean, "How did I raise a child as cruel as you?" She moved her head in long sweeps from side to side as she stood and walked behind Sarah Jane to put her hands on her shoulders. Then her eyes locked on mine as she said, "*You're* the one who doesn't know what you're talking about."

My ears burned. I lowered my eyes to the table that Dad had made. I couldn't tell whether its boomerangs were beginning or ending their journeys, but boomerangs returned to where they started, as did my words to my little sister that came back to me.

I hope I apologized enough that night. I'm still sorry, Sarah.

Life Lessons

·   The best conversations about faith involve listening and sharing, but never condescension.

·   No matter how wise you think you are, there's always more growing up to do.

THE BRADY BUNCH

During our car trip "out West" that covered six thousand miles in eighteen days, I decided that Janice and our boys deserved one splurge hotel before crossing the Great Plains. I chose the Chicago Marriott on a section of Michigan Avenue known as the Magnificent Mile. Since this hotel was the fanciest my sons had stayed in, I told them that we expected them to be on their best behavior.

When we pulled into the Marriott's motor lobby, a doorman greeted us in a snappy maroon uniform with rows of shiny brass buttons and gold shoulder epaulets. I got out to meet him and judged his smiling welcome to be professional and sincere. But when he slid open the back door on the passenger side of our Toyota Previa van, he encountered our four-year-old Rob, wedged in his car seat by an army of Beanie Babies, just as an avalanche of McDonald's wrappers, cups, and Happy Meal toys fell toward the granite block driveway and covered the toes of the doorman's shined-to-a-mirror black boots.

Before the doorman could stop himself, he said, "Jesus Christ! What do we have here? The Brady Bunch?"

Up and down the Magnificent Mile all that afternoon, Rob greeted strangers with a joyful "Jesus Christ! We're the Brady Bunch! Jesus Christ! We're the Brady Bunch!"

Life Lessons
- Unexpected chaos can make one forget one's professional training.
- Four-year-old kids are parrots.

DIXIE

When I grew up in Blacksburg, Virginia, during the fifties and sixties, most high school and college bands played "Dixie" as a second fight song. To me, "Dixie" was a welcome change from repetitions of our high school's "Onward Indians" and from Virginia Tech's "Tech Triumph." Like the opening notes of any good fight song, the heralding trumpet blares of "Dixie" brought loyal fans to their feet to yell for their team. Only a few recalcitrant Yankee transplants remained seated.

In the first Blacksburg High School pep rally after Martin Luther King, Jr. was murdered in Memphis on April 4, 1968, when our band played "Dixie," every Black student stayed seated. I was surprised. Until that day, these fellow students would stand with us whenever "Dixie" was played. But on that day, the familiar notes bowed their heads, pained their faces, crossed their arms, and held them transfixed in their seats.

I never saw a Black student stand for "Dixie" again.

◆ ◆ ◆

That my initial observance of my seated classmates surprised me is a testament to the pervasiveness of unrecognized prejudice that surrounded me in the South. Families like mine supported integration and abhorred racism. *Racist* was a word we used to describe people who preached segregation, taunted children who tried to attend better schools, and attacked civil rights workers, not good people like us.

I did not comprehend then that, like a fish that doesn't know it lives in water, I had been and was still swimming in a vast sea of white supremacy. Like so many liberal and moderate Southerners, I had adapted gills of privilege that allowed me to thrive with ease in the poisoned waters of Jim Crow. While expressing hope for a better and more equal time to come, we kept drifting in the currents of acceptance of "that's just the way things are." And by standing up and singing "Dixie" as a rallying cry, we were living proof of that acceptance.

It's taken years of reflection and soul-searching for me to understand the powerful currents of unknown prejudice that swirled around and over me, and it has taken longer for me to admit those impacts on my life.

Martin Luther King, Jr. is one of my heroes.

Life Lessons

- Beware of the presence and power of unknown prejudice around and within you.
- We are all racist; it's just a matter of degree.

DAD'S ILLNESS: PART V

A few weeks after body-surfing in the Atlantic Ocean, my seventy-eight-year-old father cracked two vertebrae sliding off his horse.

I wasn't too concerned, proud to relay his mishap to friends and colleagues that Dad was living retirement life to the max. But his recovery lingered, and rather than subsiding with physical therapy, his pain intensified. During my visits with him at his home in Mount Airy, I witnessed his excruciation at any movement of his torso. He was only comfortable lying still in his bed.

Following the physical therapist's instructions, we urged Dad to get up, sit in a chair, and take steps, asking him, "How do you expect to get better if you stay in bed all day?" When Dad succumbed to our pleading, his ordeal rendered him incapable of containing his blubbering tears. One day, after Dad got his menu of choice—fresh baby lima beans, chicken salad, and fruit—he threw it all up halfway through.

Something was wrong.

◆ ◆ ◆

A couple of weeks into Dad's illness, my three sons paid him a visit. He chose to see them one at a time. Seth was sixteen, Drew was fourteen, and Rob was five. After their private visits, I went to see Dad and found him smiling and chuckling to himself.

"What's so funny?" I asked.

"Your three sons," he said, shaking his head in cheerful disbelief. "Seth walked in and inquired how I was doing with care and sweetness. Then, Drew sat down next to me and just looked at me with those deep brown eyes that expressed everything he needed to say. And Rob," Dad said, pausing for a wincing chuckle, "Rob bounded in, put his hands on his hips, and said, 'So, Daddy Dick. Are you going to die?' Your three sons!"

◆ ◆ ◆

Back at work the next week at Presbyterian Hospital in Charlotte, I voiced my frustration to anyone who would listen. A few mornings later, a physician who specialized in spinal neurology stopped by my office. He explained that he had heard about my dad and wondered if I would like to chat. After I filled him in, he opined that, for a man who was so active, he doubted that my father's dismount would have cracked two vertebras unless something else was going on. He suggested I call Dad's doctor in Mount Airy and request a specific blood test to rule out another diagnosis. I did, and Dad's orthopedist said he would.

Two mornings later, he called to say my father was being transferred to North Carolina Baptist in Winston-Salem with a new diagnosis of multiple myeloma. There, he was admitted and began chemotherapy.

My father and mother celebrated their fiftieth anniversary in his hospital room surrounded by his wife, children, and grandchildren. With smuggled champagne, we toasted our parents' life together. Dad told Seth that he hated to miss his latest high school performance and asked him if he would sing a song for us. Seth shocked us when he stepped up and sang "Agony" from *Into the Woods*. We listened in breathless wonder as his plaintive voice brought tears that baptized our champagne.

Two weeks later, I visited Dad on my way to a board meeting in Boone. As I was leaving, I told him I would come up for a visit on the weekend. "See you Sunday," I said, not knowing it would be the last thing I would say to him.

◆　◆　◆

On Friday, Mom and Carol went to the hospital to spend most of the day with Dad. At lunchtime, they left his room to run some brief errands. In the lot where they bought Christmas wreaths, Dad's nurse rang Carol's car phone and told them that they needed to return to the hospital. By the time they got there, Dad had died. Later that day, the nurses began telling my mother and sister that, beginning early that morning, Dad had greeted every staff member who entered his room with a knowing, peaceful smile and a joyful announcement, "I'm going to die today!" On his rounds, Dad's attending oncologist debated my father's pronouncement, insisting that Dad's numbers were headed in the right direction and that he was getting better. Dad laughed at him. My father chose not to share with Mom and Carol how he had become so certain about his passing; Mom believed he wanted them gone when he died.

I learned of my father's death while driving home from Boone. I had to pull off at a rest area to catch my breath.

Janice and I sat at a picnic table and looked out at the sun's sparkles on the rippling waves of Lake Norman. It was beautiful. "My dad loved things of beauty," I said to Janice.

"Yes, he did," she said.

We drove to Mount Airy that night. Two days later, I went with Mom and my sisters to the funeral home to say our final goodbyes. It was Sunday afternoon. Walking out of the funeral home, I told Mom and my sisters, "Well, I told Dad I would see him on Sunday. And I did."

To this day, I still wonder how Dad came to know with joy and certainty about the day he was to die. Whether Dad had a feeling, a vision, a spiritual visitation, or some other heavenly revelation, I shall never know. Unless I find out someday in a place or in a way, no one on this earth can say with surety.

Life Lessons
- Faith can be an immense comfort at the time of death.
- Life's blessings flow on unique, mysterious currents of communication that we do not yet understand.

DMV PHOTO

Back in the days when North Carolina required one's physical presence at the Department of Motor Vehicles to renew a driving license, I was in line behind a woman—middle-aged, like me—who took exception to the quality of her new photo the DMV staff had just taken.

In fact, she was livid. With her voice spiking to decibels that warranted OSHA ear protection, she railed about the misuse of her tax dollars on such poor expertise, lousy equipment, and disregard for the necessity for an excellent likeness on an official government ID.

The uniformed highway patrolman absorbed her wrath like a skilled professional stoic. When the woman had to come up for air, the officer leaned forward and said, "Ma'am, in four years, you're going to love it."

Life Lessons
- When people have lived long enough, they find it hard to accept the accuracy of photographs of themselves.
- When you are listening to complaints, end by offering hope for the future.

FLUSH WATER PLANNING

A mong my duties as a lieutenant junior grade at Portsmouth Naval Hospital was oversight of housekeeping and laundry, so when word came down that a necessary repair would require cutting off the flush water system for all fifteen floors of the hospital for several hours, I wondered how we would cope without an ability to flush a single toilet.

The planning for this eventuality was meticulous. Meetings and memos cascaded down the chain of command. Many good minds focused on minimizing disruption by maximizing advanced communication. My initial worries morphed into pride for being a part of an impressive effort. I took comfort in learning that the potable (drinking, bathing) water system would remain intact, extra nursing staff would be on the floors, and the repair would only take about an hour and a half. During that time, the toilets in our fifteen-story tower were not to be used. Staff and visitors could use working toilets in other campus buildings, and patients would be provided with bedpans.

As the selected day and time approached—Friday at 1300 hours, or 1:00 p.m.—I paced the tiled hallways, trying to loosen the knot of flittering nerves in my stomach. *We have a good plan*, I told myself. And we did. When the flush water ceased flowing, I heard not one complaint. The repair went without a hitch, and after an hour and a half, word came that the flush water pipes were set to reopen any minute. Pride that all of our planning had paid off so well swelled my chest and stretched the fabric around the buttons on my uniform shirt.

Or so it seemed.

Within seconds, geysers began to erupt from the ground-floor toilets and drains next to the main elevator bank. The force of the water blew toilet seats to the ceiling and then ate holes in the acoustic tiles. Manhole covers in the courtyard rose as if Neptune was putting on a magic act. A shin-deep river flooded the main hallway from the front entrance to the hospital's largest elevator bank.

Our housekeeping force sprang into action and hustled to the coursing river with water evacuation vacuums and mops, but the flood overwhelmed their efforts. When I waded into the water, I knew there was no "sucking up" this quantity of liquid—we had to redirect it. I directed our staff to ditch their vacuums and mops and start building dikes and levees with our linen supplies to channel the water into the courtyard or toward the loading dock doors. Within minutes, the water began flowing out of the building.

The teamwork in those crucial moments filled me with immense pride. Every member of our housekeeping team, both civilian and naval personnel, had pitched to minimize the ill effects of whatever had just occurred. When the water from the toilets slowed to a trickle, our mops and vacuums returned. Smiles broke across stern faces. Pats fell on backs, and our team's success made us giddy that our pants were soaked to our knees. We had done it.

◆ ◆ ◆

Among the crowd of onlookers, many of whom were relief staff reporting for the three-to-eleven shift and now waited for egress to the stairwells and elevators, was a physician, a lieutenant commander irritated that he couldn't get to his floor. He marched up to me and said in a booming voice, "I cannot believe that *you* picked this time to clean the floors! At change of shift!" He spewed other words that, while I cannot recall them exactly, I know conveyed that he was dressing down what had to be the dumbest officer in the command.

All work stopped. Silence descended as my cleanup team of heroes waited to hear what I would say.

They didn't have to wait long. I lost it. In a voice as loud as the physician had used, I said, "Well, you can just eat shit . . . sir!"

Then I wheeled around to stomp off in indignation and slammed straight into the chest of our commanding officer, Rear Admiral William J. Jacoby, Jr.

I heard a few gasps as I stepped back. Admiral Jacoby was known for his tell-it-like-it-is, no-nonsense style and short-fused temper. Before I could apologize, Admiral Jacoby's powerful voice said, "Carry on, Mr. Howerton."

"You," Admiral Jacoby said, pointing to the now wide-eyed doctor, "in my office, *now!*"

Later, I learned that our CO witnessed most of our team's response. I was told that he smiled as he watched us work before inviting that doctor to his office, from which the young physician exited a few pounds lighter. In fairness, the physician may have just arrived on the scene, oblivious to the magnitude of the initial flooding.

◆ ◆ ◆

After all that planning, what went wrong? Our planners had failed to consider the innate curiosity of human beings and their need to prove things to themselves.

While our staff had absorbed the preparatory communications, many of them decided to conduct a personal test by flushing unused, clean toilets to prove to themselves, "Yep, they don't work." While those tested toilets did not flush, their valves stayed locked open because normally functioning valves depend on water flow to turn them off at the end of a flushing cycle. When the water came back on, hundreds of toilets flushed simultaneously, overloading the drainage pipe capacity. That flushed water sought its most direct and lowest exit—in this case, the visitor restrooms on the main corridor adjacent to the main elevator bank. A one-time torrent came at us with the power of fifteen stories of hydrologic physics.

Months later, Admiral Jacoby asked through proper channels if I would be interested in serving as his aide.

Life Lessons
- Excellent planning helps a good team perform well, but the response to a crisis can bring out its best.
- Before you publicly criticize something that seems obvious, get the whole story.

SIZE SMALL

From the day that my mother delivered a ten-and-a-half-pound me, I've never worn a small anything. As a kid, Mom bought my clothes in a size named "husky." In the eighth grade, I learned the word "Butterball" was not relegated solely to a brand of Thanksgiving turkeys. Wide-hipped and slow, I played offensive line in football. After tossing the discus at track meets, I ran on our Fat Man's Relay team, a novelty that prompted guffawing from the fleet gazelles who ran real races.

My size followed me into marriage and fatherhood. Our first son, Seth, was one of twenty-six born on the evening shift in the factory-efficient delivery system of Portsmouth Naval Hospital. Janice didn't get to hold her son for another twenty-four hours, as was hospital protocol at the time. For the birth of our second son, Drew, Janice insisted on more participative Lamaze and LeBoyer experiences, which were not hard to arrange since, by then, I was the administrator of a small county hospital in Oxford, North Carolina.

Janice labored for twenty hours to deliver Seth, but Drew came so fast that when she was rushed to the delivery room, there was no time to move her from the gurney to the delivery table. In my rush to play my part in this birthing miracle, I grabbed the first set of green surgical scrubs I could find, yanked them on, and ran into the delivery room just in time to catch Drew. A transcendent peace settled over me as I lowered him into a tub of warm water and gently bathed him for several peaceful moments. Then I handed him to Janice and witnessed the magic of bonding between mother and child.

When Janice and Drew were rolled out of the delivery suite, it was time for me to put my suit and tie back on. But there was a problem. No matter how much I pulled and tugged, I could not budge the scrubs' cotton fabric from my skin. It was as if the threads had grown into me. To this day, I have no idea how I managed to get the scrubs on without tearing them in half.

To free myself, I had to cut those scrubs off with surgical scissors. After that, I could see the tag that read, "Ladies Size Small."

Life Lessons
- Birth is a wonder to behold.
- Adrenaline is a powerful drug.

ONLY ONE COWBOY

The Granville Hospital Board of Trustees approved me as their administrator because they had contracted with a hospital management company that would provide an experienced professional with whom I could consult should my twenty-seven-year-old thinking fall short. After a few weeks on the job, I faced a problem that I had no idea how to handle.

After stewing and fretting that I should be able to figure things out on my own and imagining how embarrassing it would be to have to admit that I needed help so soon, I finally picked up the phone and called my area vice president.

I was lucky that John Carlisle answered the phone right away. John loved to help people. He was a great listener and exuded a calm, caring presence. He declared my apology for bothering him as unnecessary and then permitted me to ramble on about the crisis, which seemed of utmost importance to me. He thanked me for calling him and assured me that that was what he was there for.

After a few clarifying questions, he asked me to articulate the alternative courses of action, which I did. Then he asked me what I was going to do.

"What do *you* think I should do?" I asked.

John emitted a slight chuckle. I could see him in my mind nodding and smiling.

"Richard," he said. "There can be only one cowboy on that horse. And you are in the saddle. I'm confident that you'll make a good decision. Let me know what you decide to do, and I will back you up."

Then he hung up.

Life Lessons
- Sometimes, letting someone figure things out on their own can be the catalyst for professional development.
- Asking for help when you need it is a strength, not a weakness.

ROTO-ROOTER MAN

Our first house came with a septic tank. All I knew about it was that it meant we couldn't hook up to the city's sewage system. The previous owners were meticulous in their maintenance, leaving us a three-ring binder of instructions to mentor our nascent homeownership. Perhaps they assumed we knew that there were certain commodities of sanitation that should never enter a septic tank.

The plumbing worked fine, so I gave it no further thought. Not, that is, until our wastewater began creeping across our garage floor, oozing out of the lowest drain in the house.

That wasn't the first thing to go wrong that weekend in the summer of 1976.

Our overnight guests were already enduring the oppressive heat and humidity of Tidewater, Virginia, thanks to our air-conditioning conking out the night before. Wide-open windows and fans offered little relief.

Our guests suggested we try calling Roto-Rooter, and thirty minutes after I did, into our driveway pulled a red truck, out of which unfolded a lanky, happy creature, who bounded up the front steps and announced his presence would solve our problems. His bubbling demeanor belied his dark complexion and sunken cheeks. After thanking him for coming, the Roto-Rooter man ran back to his truck and donned a brown jumpsuit stained with something wet.

The Roto-Rooter man located our septic tank by probing our backyard with a long steel rod, educating me on how a septic system worked. During my tutorial on the merits of bacteria to break down human excrement, he stopped, beamed, and shouted, "I found your tank!" with robust enthusiasm as if he'd discovered the Fountain of Youth. He attacked our earth with a spade until a concrete surface came into view. Then, he knelt down and pried open a lid of cement.

The stench hit me first. I had to step back to regain my balance. Then the breeze took the odor inside our house, eliciting groans from female and male voices.

The Roto-Rooter man lowered his head to get a better look and the visceral soup below. Then he leaned back on his heels, rolled up his sleeve, bowed back down, and plunged his bare arm into the muck. Seconds later he pulled his arm out, sat back, lifted his arm toward me, and said with glee, "Here's your problem!"

"What is that?" I asked about the dripping concoction in his hand.

"Sanitary goods!" he declared, smiling all the while.

Life Lessons
- Homeownership is an educational experience.
- A human being who loves his or her work can be a joy to behold.

RALPH'S RATTLESNAKE RANCH

My father was an intelligent man who tried to learn from his mistakes. Wanting to avoid another radiator eruption in the middle of a cross-country trip, he acquired a preventive overhaul of our Buick's five-year-old cooling system a week before our departure. He brought me along as a witness. The mechanic praised my father's forethought because he found numerous radiator leaks to patch. As an added precaution to reduce stress on the new patches, he replaced the factory-specified fifteen-pound pressure radiator cap with one of lesser ten-pound resistance. It seemed logical at the time.

Either because our trusty old tent came back in shreds from Europe two years before or because my sisters and I were grown teenagers and needed more room, for the first (and only) time, Dad borrowed a camping luxury—an Apache trailer with a fold-out tent. With the Apache in tow, we trekked through the Midwest, across the Great Plains, the Rockies, the Sierra Nevada, and Lake Tahoe, and then to San Francisco, where we saw bushels of flowers in long hair during the 1967 Summer of Love. Big Sur to Disneyland was next, before heading back.

◆ ◆ ◆

The first leg of our trip home was crossing the Mohave Desert. In the July heat, our Buick performed well for about three hours; then I heard Mom say, "Dick, something's wrong. A red light just came on."

Before Dad could respond, our Buick shook and emitted a loud metallic growl. "Pull off here," Dad said as an exit materialized out of the heat mirage. Mom aimed the car toward the only building around, a gas station named Ralph's.

As we coasted toward the pumps, our car died amid a cloud of steam. We were not alone. A gang of Hells Angels were topping off their tanks and seemed curious about our plight but then roared off without more than a few poor-you headshakes. As I got out of the car, I noticed a sign that read "Ralph's Rattlesnake Ranch" with an arrow pointing out back.

Ralph's diagnosis was a blown head gasket that would require rebuilding the engine, which was beyond his ability to repair. Until the wrecker arrived, I wandered into his "ranch," a trail through chicken wire cages of sleeping vipers nestled amid brush and cacti. Despite the heat, goose bumps rose on my forearms.

The nearest garage capable of such work was in Las Vegas, eighty miles away. Ralph called a friend with a tow truck, who quoted a fare of a dollar a mile payable in cash, which consumed all remaining paper money and most coins among our family. When Carol and I realized the tow truck was air-conditioned (our cars never were), we hopped in, leaving our poor little sister, Sarah Jane, to experience the brunt of Mom and Dad's heated dialogue as the tow truck towed our Buick towing an Apache.

◆ ◆ ◆

Being a Baptist preacher, Las Vegas was not on Dad's itinerary for an overnight stay. The repair would take three days, and Dad had to call and tell the chairman of his board of deacons that he wouldn't be back to preach on Sunday. Dad's second call was to another member of his church, a banker, to arrange a two-thousand-dollar wire transfer. I imagined their conversation might have gone something like, "Now, let me get this straight, preacher. You need me to transfer two grand for your 'emergency' in Las Vegas?" Dad's Gulf credit card covered our stay at the Holiday Inn on the edge of town next to some new place called Caesars Palace. At the Flamingo across the street, James Brown and Flip Wilson were playing, but all that did was make me furious that I was too young and broke to go to the show.

Back at the garage, the mechanics rebuilt our Buick's engine. If there was a debate about whether to replace the old patched radiator or not, I never knew. We drove out of Vegas with new head gaskets, our veteran radiator, and, unbeknownst to us, a new pressure cap to replace the cautionary ten-pound cap that the Virginia radiator expert installed before our trip. Perhaps in the hellish heat and steam at Ralph's Rattlesnake Ranch, someone deemed that substitute cap superfluous. Who knows? We know now the Vegas mechanics replaced the missing radiator cap with what the specs called for—a full fifteen-pound pressure one, putting those patches at risk.

Our Buick's rebuilt engine purred all the way to downtown Anniston, Alabama, where a cloud of steam once again rose from our hood. A service station mechanic delivered the verdict: the radiator's patches had blown off.

Dad bought a new radiator, and we made it home four days late.

Life Lessons
- Scrimping on maintenance will cost you in the long run.
- When someone jerry-rigs a solution, however well-intended, the rationale of that creativity may not be obvious to the next person who has to fix it.

FLYING WITH A MORTICIAN

Returning from a meeting in Orlando, I was worried that my flight back to Charlotte might be canceled. Tornadoes were popping up in Georgia and South Carolina. Outside, the tarmac was ponding from driving rain. But I was surprised when I heard the announcement that it was time to board our plane.

When the last passenger took a seat, the pilot's voice came over the intercom and communicated his eagerness to take advantage of a "window of departure." Our packed plane taxied near the end of the runaway, where the pilot told us that all flights had been suspended until an intense local storm passed over us, but we would hold our current position rather than return to the gate and risk losing our "window."

In those days, it was not uncommon to strike up a conversation with passengers who sat around you. By nightfall, the plane was abuzz with nervous exchanges about the weather and odds of missing connections if we didn't leave through our "window." Seated on my left was a woman about my age, tall like me, dark brunette, wearing a business suit. Having shared that I worked in healthcare, she volunteered that she was a mortician in her family's funeral business in Minneapolis. I had never met a female mortician, but I was eager to share that both my grandfather and great-grandfather had owned a funeral home in Durham, North Carolina. Soon we knew that both of us had played hide-and-seek in the coffin showroom. What were the odds?

Our pilot knew his stuff because after the local storm passed, air traffic control allowed flights to resume, and we were first to depart. Before he got the wheels up, the roughest air that I had ever experienced before or since slammed us and continued to for the entire flight. As a frequent flier, I had been on some scary flights, but this one was unique in its relentlessness. Bumps and bounces morphed into plunges and jolts that banged bones and whipped necks. Cinched seatbelts bruised hips as they held torsos from jamming heads into the overhead fuselage.

Somehow, we persevered until the flight attendant announced preparations for landing. Our descent was as harrowing as the flight, but when the pilot pulled out of his runway approach and throttled up for another pass, several passengers groaned. Some began to cry. After the pilot aborted his second attempt to land, I heard praying. Someone was reciting the twenty-third Psalm.

As the pilot circled for his third attempt, I felt the mortician's shoulder lean into mine. Instead of retreating as I would normally do, I leaned in. Then, her leg pressed along mine from thigh to knee to shin to ankle, and I kept mine in place. There, we stayed without saying a word. With contact came a sense of stability, as if we were trying to anchor ourselves in midair from whatever might come next. I leaned my head back and confessed that I never imagined

I would die sitting, sides touching sides, with a mortician from Minneapolis. But at least we wouldn't die alone without a human's touch.

The wheels struck runway pavement. Reversing engines howled, and we began to slow. Passengers cheered. Some wept. The mortician and I shifted in our seats. Normal spacing returned between us. Taxiing was uneventful, deplaning, routine.

In the concourse the mortician and I smiled our goodbyes, which I took as an acknowledgment that we'd never forget our wild ride together and our sharing the power of comfort a near stranger can give. No words were exchanged. Not even names.

Life Lessons
- The simple touch of one human can do what words cannot in times of danger.
- Even strangers have the power to comfort one another.

A PICK IN YOUR EYE

After work one summer evening, I decided to mow the lawn before Janice and Rob returned for dinner. While doing my push-pull routine around the buried poles of our backyard swing set, something struck my right eye with a *thunk*. I staggered back, horrified that I had done what mothers warn kids not to do—I had put my eye out.

With a palm over my socket, I stumbled over to the back steps and sat down. My lawnmower was still running. After a while, I dared to open my eye and was shocked that I could see things, but the swirl of black specks and something that looked like a dragon with a long swooping, swirling tail could not be good.

After washing the dust off in the shower, I drove myself to the Presbyterian Hospital Emergency Room. There, the doctor told me that I was lucky the stone had neither hit my iris nor caused a detached retina. But two weeks later, a gray shade began lowering over my sight in my injured eye. My retina was detaching itself.

Surgery followed to restore and preserve my eye's vision, consisting of a scleral buckle procedure (a belt of silicone cinched around my eyeball) and an injection of a gas bubble. My recovery at home required sleeping or lying still on my side for twenty hours a day for one week so that the bubble could float up and press the retina back into place. During that first week of recuperation, any back-and-forth eye movement was excruciating, so there was no reading or watching TV. The only thing I could do was listen, talk, eat, or sleep. Book tapes were a godsend. Then came two more weeks away from work.

My retinologist explained that the retina is an extension of the optic nerve, which is a part of the brain, and when the retina undergoes trauma or surgery, it shuts the brain down to maximize/mandate rest and recovery. My surgery and recovery were successful. As expected, a trauma-induced cataract developed six months later, requiring more surgery and a new lens implant.

Three years later, my left eye decided to get in on the fun, detaching its retina spontaneously. More surgery, stillness, cataract removal, laser tweaks, and lens implant followed, all successful. I feel truly fortunate—without modern medicine and nine eye surgeries, I would be blind in both eyes.

One afternoon, during my recovery from my second detached retina surgery, my retinologist called me and asked for a favor: Would I be willing to speak to one of his detached retina patients about what to expect from the surgery and recovery because his patient was in denial of what was to come? I told him I would be happy to.

A few hours later, I got a call from a man who, after a curt thank-you for taking the time to speak with him, launched into all the reasons that he was too busy and too valuable to his wealth management company to drop everything and take three weeks away from work.

"How could it possibly take that long?" he asked. "I just can't take that much time off."

"OK. Do you know what a geologist's pick is?" I asked him.

"A what?"

"You know, one of those hammers with a tapered point on one end that geologists use to split rocks?"

"I guess," he said in a tone that I could tell he wondered what geology had to do with anything.

"Well, if you try to read or even look at a computer monitor or a TV screen that first week, it will feel like someone's hitting your eye with a geologist's pick."

"Really?"

"Yes, really. Look, I've been through this not once but twice, and it was like that both times. A couple of days after surgery, you might be able to take, not make, some phone calls. Reading is out of the question."

There was a long silence.

"Oh. I guess I'm going to have to make some different plans."

"Good idea. Want to borrow some book tapes?"

Life Lessons
- Listen to your surgeon, and be realistic about how long your recovery should take.
- When you mow the lawn, wear protective glasses.

WEIGH BOY PART II: JOE

The summer I was promoted from laboring in an asphalt plant to the shack that weighed trucks, I was most often in the company of Joe, a master driver of a front loader and everything else with wheels or treads on the quarry hill. Joe loaded stone into the beds of dump trucks on demand. He was a wizard at wielding the scoop of his front loader, more often than not coming within two hundred pounds on a five-ton order.

Dark-haired, stocky, and strong, Joe was a slow talker when he spoke at all. A false first impression might lead one to doubt his intelligence. Joe saw no need to fill silences with words. He kept his Vietnam experiences to himself, along with his opinions about most things. When he was not driving something, he sat with me in the weigh station at a scavenged dinette table and read whatever was around until the phone rang in another order. As long as our response was prompt, the hill boss didn't care if we spent most of our day sitting around reading, waiting for something to happen.

We read the *Blacksburg Sun*, the *Montgomery News Messenger*, the *Roanoke Times*, and *Newsweek*, then graduated to paperback novels. Joe read them faster than I could. He liked *The Godfather* and Don Corleone's making offers you can't refuse. *Rabbit Run* made him opine, "That Rabbit better just keep on running." After *Herzog*, he said, "Saul Bellow sure likes him some Chicago architecture."

I'm not sure why, but Joe took up for me when one of the "independents"—truck owners for private hire—demanded that I add to his loaded weight by pressing my finger on the scale and fudging his payload. When I hesitated, Joe said, "Leave him be." And he did.

◆ ◆ ◆

When I arrived the morning of the biggest state highway job of that summer, over a dozen dump trucks were lined up at the asphalt plant. I took my post at the scales, and the plant began belching out load after load into waiting trucks stationed under the trestle and steel framing that supported the hot mixing tanks above. Joe manned a bulldozer that day, piloting its blade in wide swaths, shoving masses of stone and sand into the mouths of conveyors.

The last truck in line that morning had a rookie behind the wheel. On the first day of his first job since soldiering in Vietnam, he fell in line and played follow-the-leader. He watched the drivers in front of him coat their truck beds with fuel oil pumped out of a container, not unlike ones that sprayed insecticide on shrubbery. The new guy inherited an empty canister, so he refilled it from the parked ancient tanker trailer like he had watched the other drivers do. But the rookie opened the wrong spigot. Instead of filling his canister with fuel oil, he filled it with gasoline, coated his truck bed, drove under the trestle, and waited for his load. When the scorching asphalt hit his truck bed, flames leaped to the top of the four-story tower in one big *whoosh*.

While we learned of the rookie's missteps later, through my window I witnessed the flames engulf the plant while sitting on my stool less than a hundred feet away. Seconds later, I saw the driver get out of his truck and run. He wasn't alone. Everyone working near the plant bolted. I phoned the boss's trailer and shouted what I was seeing.

A quarry driver came in and yelled, "Get the hell out of here, Weigh Boy! This whole place could blow!"

I should have listened to him, but the conflagration transfixed me. As the fire melted rubber hoses and electric cables snapped in bursts of white sparks, the driverless dump truck lurched forward. *How could that be? Something had to be pushing it. But what?* Then a bulldozer blade pushing the truck emerged out of the smoke, and next, metal treads, and finally, its driver, Joe, his head ducking beneath the flames.

"Joe! What are you doing?" I shouted.

Joe's face looked fierce; his jaw clenched, his feet pounding pedals, his arms pumping levers as his bulldozer continued to shove the burning dump truck, its braked tires gouging rows of gravel as it moved away from the trestle into an open space. With the source of flames removed, the plant tower fire began to die down, but every inch of the truck blazed. The bulldozer stopped and backed away. Joe hopped down, ran to his front loader, zoomed to the nearest gravel pile, rammed his scoop into it, wheeled back toward the blazing rig with his scoop extended high, and dumped his full load of gravel onto the flames. Joe made trip after trip, heaping stones until the truck disappeared. But the limestone caught fire, and flames continued to burst through the pile in sporadic flares.

The firetrucks arrived and extinguished the flames, but the mound of sooty limestone smoked for days.

◆ ◆ ◆

Throughout the rest of the week, the story of the rookie's fire and Joe's heroics was told and retold. Joe's reward was extra vacation, which he saved for Christmas to be with his wife and kids. But as the days wore on, Joe's feats became old news, and to some of the hardcore vets, Joe's selfless act was foolish.

With the asphalt plant out of commission, quarried stone was the only thing for sale on the hill. Joe and I read most days of the next two weeks. One afternoon, Joe decided that his front loader could use a grease job. I watched as he extended his scoop out on its arms, revealing two long, smooth steel cylinders. Joe inserted safety chocks on the cylinders to keep the scoop high in place, making it safe for him to work in its shade. The telephone bell mounted on the side of the weigh station summoned me. Trotting to the phone, I guessed it was probably an order for "crush and run," the most common stone purchased. It was, and I yelled the tonnage out to Joe from the doorway.

Joe didn't answer, which was not unusual. I couldn't see Joe at work because a mound of stone blocked my view. I grabbed a broom and swept loose stones off the weighing platform, more to kill time than ensure an accurate scale weight. Then I went inside the station to wait for the truck.

A few minutes later, one of the quarry drivers wanted Joe for something and asked where he was. I told him. Seconds later, the man burst back through the door and yelled, "Call an ambulance! Joe's hurt!" Then he ran back in Joe's direction.

I called 911, but when the operator asked for the address, I couldn't tell her what it was. I gave her directions while fumbling around, searching for the address on the paperwork I used to weigh trucks. I found it, but not without causing precious seconds to tick away. Then I phoned the hill boss, filled him in, and asked that he call 911 too to make sure an ambulance was on the way. The quarry driver was with Joe, so I decided to stay by the phone should more emergency calls be necessary.

Several long minutes later, the hill boss came down with the ambulance. Another front loader came and lifted the scoop off Joe's chest so the EMTs could race Joe to the trauma center at Roanoke Memorial.

The hill boss told me that the safety chocks had come loose, and the scoop crushed Joe's chest, pinning him to the ground.

Joe died later that day.

For a reason that I will never understand, I could not bring myself to attend Joe's funeral. I lost the opportunity to pay my last respects and to tell his wife how much I admired Joe. My absence from Joe's service is something that I have regretted and bear in shame to this day.

The day that one of the independents called Joe stupid for not knowing how to chock a cylinder was my last day on the hill.

Life Lessons
- Heroes put the needs of others before their own and let their actions speak for themselves.
- You only have one chance to go to someone's funeral.

JOEY'S TOOTH

One afternoon after work, I turned into our Charlotte driveway, expecting to see my sons and the neighborhood kids playing four square or shooting baskets at the rim I had lowered to accommodate their slam-dunk height. The driveway was empty.

Inside, I found Janice at our kitchen sink with her arm around Joey, a nine-year-old boy from Arizona who was in town visiting his father. There was a glass bowl of milk on the counter with something in it.

"Hey. What are you doing?"

Janice kept her back to me as she wiped off Joey's face. She spoke with a quiet assurance. "Joey knocked his front tooth out on the basketball rim. He doesn't have a dentist. I can't reach Joey's father, so I called Dr. Adams, and he said we had to find the tooth and then call him back. So, we looked and looked, but we were looking for something too small. We ended up finding it farther away, in the grass, way over next to the neighbor's backyard fence, and it was huge. Drew remembered reading that we should wash it and keep it in milk." I looked back at the bowl. "I called

Dr. Adams back, and he told me that I had to shove Joey's tooth back in place and meet him in his office. His office is closed, so I'll be his assistant to help glue it back in. So that's what I'm about to do."

My jaw dropped, and Janice added, "And Joey's being *such* a big boy."

I felt woozy. I was stuck on "shove the tooth back in." I took a quick breath and asked, "You're going to do what?"

"You heard me. Dr. Adams said time is of the essence. Now, here we go, Joey."

And she did exactly what she said she was going to do.

Years later, we saw Joey when he visited the neighborhood as a young man. He was a Marine and a Golden Gloves boxer. His wide smile flashed that front tooth, still implanted right where Janice had shoved it.

Life Lessons
- Caring for someone may require quick thinking and leaping into action when time is of the essence.
- Mothers can do amazing things.

LEXINGTON REVISITED

In 1962, my father took me to Lexington, Virginia, for the first time. I was in the fifth grade. Like my hometown of Blacksburg, Lexington was a college town—a two-college town, hosting both the Virginia Military Institute (VMI) and Washington and Lee University (W&L). The lore of Virginia's history and its role in the Civil War was ubiquitous, practically oozing out of the town's brick mortar and down its stark white Doric columns.

The Virginia public school system had me well versed in the legends of George Washington, Stonewall Jackson, and, of course, Robert E. Lee, the latter of whom was presented to us as the perfect Southern gentleman and the best commander in military history. What classrooms taught me was reinforced on playgrounds, among groups of adults, and on the walls of friends' houses, where paintings of Civil War battle scenes and the Battle Flag of the Confederacy and etched portraits of Lee himself often hung.

In Lexington that first time, Dad drove me by the VMI cannons and Stonewall Jackson's house, but at Washington and Lee, we stopped and went into Lee Chapel. There,

I saw a white marble statue of a reclining Robert E. Lee where an altar should be. Confederate flags flanked him. The hushed silence morphed my reverence into awe that this sacred place was a house of worship for both God and Robert E. Lee. Was there any difference? Dad, being a horse lover, made sure to take me into the chapel's small basement museum to see the skeleton of Lee's trusted stead, Traveler, his hide bundled and laid to rest at his front hooves.

◆ ◆ ◆

A word about my father. My family's oral history included how Dad, when serving as statewide minister to Southern Baptists in all of North Carolina colleges and universities, was fired for hiring a Black minister to serve the state's historically Black colleges. My mother told this story to convey to my sisters and me that my father believed that all of God's children were equal and that he favored integration and hoped that the segregated culture of the South would someday change. I knew that Dad admired the work of Martin Luther King, Jr. and other courageous and righteous civil rights leaders. I had heard about the time when Southern Baptists were meeting in Atlantic City, and Dad saw the elder Reverend Martin Luther King Sr. sitting in a café alone and asked if he could join him. They chatted for hours about the admirable leadership of the minister's son.

Looking back, why did my father take me to Lexington to visit that chapel shrine built for Robert E. Lee? Was it for the sake of history? Was it a nod to the reconciliatory stature Lee had gained after the war? That I, like him, was supposed to revere the leader of the Army of Northern Virginia, I did not question, not at that time in my life. Was it all of the above or something else?

In my teenage years, television displayed the personal trauma inflicted upon nonviolent civil rights protesters. I witnessed the pain and anger in the eyes of the Blacks I knew in the days following Martin Luther King, Jr.'s assassination. I came to see myself as an enlightened white Southern young man. During my college years, as president of my fraternity, I took pride that we initiated five Black brothers—we were the first fraternity to do so—and I believed that what Sam Cooke sang about in "A Change Is Gonna Come" was here and now. In 1980, I refused an invitation to join a country club because that club had just denied the membership application of a Black businessman on my hospital board who would have been the club's first African American member. In 1985, I won the Charlotte Writer's Club competition for my article, "Dancing on a Razor with Martin Luther King, Jr.," in which I thanked God for MLK and his championing and achieving civil rights so my sons wouldn't have to live in the separate-but-unequal culture of my childhood.

So why, in 1987, when Janice and I decided to take Seth and Drew to see Washington, DC, did I decide that they too needed to stop by Lexington and see what I did as a kid? When I visited Lee Chapel for a second time, I felt like I had walked into a sucker punch. My sons' eyes stared at me, questioning why I had brought them to this odd place. And why had busloads of school kids, half of whom were Black, been brought there too in the state-tax-paid yellow school buses of the Commonwealth of Virginia? The site of African American and white kids parading past Lee's reclined body on his white marble bed was beyond tragic irony. It was a personal epiphany. I was naive about the extent of my brainwashing that I held on to the need to take my sons to Lexington as my father had me. To myself, I admitted that the South was not through with me, and I understood that the culture of white supremacy could leech out within us even amid self-congratulatory deception.

I hope that I have come a long way from that day in Lexington with my sons. I have read, talked, prayed, studied, and posted about tolerance and reconciliation. We have a Black Lives Matter sign in our yard. And I have a long way to go. I always will. We always will.

Whether we know it or not.

Postscript: Earlier in my life, the books *Blood Done Sign My Name* and *The Blood of Emmitt Till* by Timothy B. Tyson profoundly influenced my development. More recently, in 2020 and 2021, I read books about our nation's battle with itself over the true history of enslaving Africans and the war that tried to keep them that way.

I have read discourses about why it is so difficult to talk about our unknown and unconfronted bigotry, racism, and white supremacist history, the extent of which not only we are often unaware but also can anger many of us even to suggest we might need to have a dialogue about it. The books I have read during these years include the following:

- *White Fragility* by Robin DiAngelo
- *Frederick Douglas: Prophet of Freedom* by David W. Blight
- *The Color of Compromise: The Truth about the American Church's Complicity in Racism* by Jemar Tisby
- *Caste* by Isabel Wilkerson
- *Begin Again* by Eddie Glaude, Jr.
- *These Truths: A History of the United States* by Jill Lepore
- *Robert E. Lee and Me: A Southerner's Reckoning with the Myth of the Lost Cause* by Ty Seidule

I highly recommend all of these books.

Regarding Lexington, US Army Colonel (Retired) Seidule's book was most apropos. Seidule was raised in Virginia like me and exposed to the same Virginia history. A decade younger than I, he attended W&L, where he continued to adore Robert E. Lee and to believe the myth of the Lost Cause of the Confederacy, learning its tenets as I did. One of the most often tenets espoused is that the Civil War was not about slavery but states' rights. Seidule taught history at West Point, and from his book I learned that the best rejoinder to proponents of the states' rights argument is written in black and white right in the Constitution of the Confederate States of America. Article 1, Section 9 (4) of that document says, "No bill of attainer, ex post facto law, or law denying or impairing the right of property in negro slaves shall be passed." In other words, Confederate states did not have states' rights when it came to whether it was legal or illegal to enslave Black human beings—the Constitution of the Confederate States of America required the right to own slaves in every one of its states. It was not a state's option. So much for states' rights.

Seidule now sees the Civil War for what it was—a war of rebellion to preserve the right to enslave Africans. As I do now. Only three years ago, I confessed aloud for the first time to sixty men at church, "While I owe my life to my two great-grandfathers who fought for the Confederacy and survived, I thank God that the South lost the war." It took much more out of me to say that than it should have. And it took way too long.

It was easier to post those words on Facebook the following week. It's easier still to write them now.

The truth gets easier to tell.

Life Lessons

- People don't always know who or what they really are.
- A constant pursuit of knowledge, no matter how surprised or regretful you may be at the truth you uncover about yourself, is the only way to keep growing your soul.

THIS LIFE AND ONE MORE

In moments of trial and stress, my grandmother Ora used to say, "This life and one more!" It was her way to both blow off steam and express her faith in the ultimate new life hereafter that awaited her. My mother often chose to quote my grandmother after some of my youthful foibles. I found myself quoting them both five days after March 29, 2009.

Six months earlier, Mom was planning a family reunion to honor the memory of her older sister, Valeria. All my first cousins on the Jackson side of the family came together for perhaps one last time. They were unanimous in voicing how good Mom looked, and I agreed. Mom was proud of her recent slenderer figure, thanks to Lean Cuisine.

But my mother kept losing weight, and just before Christmas, her physician diagnosed her with colon cancer. Mom opted for surgery, saying that she wanted to be around to see the birth of her first great-grandchild, Nora, and the marriage of my son Drew to Lydia in the fall. In his post-operation remarks to us, her surgeon told us the operation was as successful as it could have been and that he had removed as much of the invasive tumor as possible, but he couldn't get it all. He recommended she follow up with an oncologist.

Mom went home within a few weeks. She declined the oncology referral, having promised herself that she would never have chemotherapy and radiation after nursing her older and younger sisters with their cancers. Our son, Seth, volunteered to stay with Mom for six weeks. Then Mom's appetite began to diminish. Nausea followed, and soon, she needed around-the-clock care.

When her primary physician suggested it was time for hospice, the task of telling Mom fell to me.

◆　◆　◆

It was a March morning filled with the radiant light of a low winter sun. Mom was in her den, a room with yellow walls displaying pictures of mountains that Dad had painted. On one wall framed photographed faces of family members watched over us. I sat on the side of Mom's hospital bed and took her hand in mine, wondering how I should begin.

Mom spoke first. "I just don't know why I'm so sick."

I took her to mean that she couldn't understand her recent and consistent inability to keep down anything that she ate. I opted for the truth. "Mom, it's because your intestines are shutting down," I whispered.

Her eyes widened. In a clear voice, she said, "What? I thought I would have a year or two." I just looked into her eyes. Moments of silence passed. Then she said, "That changes everything. I should never have had that surgery."

"But Mom, don't you remember? You said you wanted to see your first great-grandchild, and you did. You held her in your arms. Your decision to have surgery allowed that to happen." I didn't mention her other goal of being present for Drew's wedding, but my heart's ache projected her future absence. Then I added, "Now, it's time for hospice to help us care for you."

Mom closed her eyes. She had nothing more to say.

A few days later, when I was alone with Mom, I asked her if there was anything she wished to share with me. She replied with a simple, "No."

◆　◆　◆

As I wrote Mom's obituary with the help of my sisters, I thought about what I would say at her memorial service. I wished Mom had blessed me with some final pearls of wisdom in her final days. Then it dawned on me that she already had, during our dawn talks around her kitchen table, in her thoughtful handwritten letters, and most of all by her living example long before we knew anything about her terminal illness. At that moment, Grandmother Ora's and Mom's words, "This life and one more," echoed in my mind with a new ring of truth about her clarity and conviction of her faith in my heart. Like her mother, Ora, Mom lived her faith in service to others, comforted in her belief that there was much more to come.

"This life and one more" were the last words I said in my eulogy to Sarah Jackson Howerton on April 3, 2009. She was eighty-six.

Life Lessons
- Faith can be a great comfort at the time of one's passing.
- All things must pass—but what about souls?

A HUGO MOTHER'S SON

In late September of 1989, Hurricane Hugo's Category 5 winds demolished the Virgin Islands before slamming into the South Carolina coast north of Charleston. Then, a meteorologic phenomenon of aligned weather fronts "sling-shotted" the monster storm inland toward the Charlotte metro area, where most residents were unprepared for sustained hurricane-force winds blowing two hundred miles from the coast.

But not Janice. My wife was a veteran of Hurricane Hazel in her hometown of inland Wilson, North Carolina, and she'd witnessed tree-splitting wind shears in Chesapeake, so when she heard weather forecasters warning that trash cans and other unanchored objects should be secured, she sprang into action. By midnight, she had us in the safest area of the house on mattresses, with flashlights, a portable radio, water bottles, and Oreos. Our three sons bounced between adventurous enthusiasm, fear, and certainty that their parents' paranoia had commandeered their sanity. The administrator on call at Presbyterian Hospital, Mark Farmer, called me to report that he was already on-site, helping prepare for whatever Hugo delivered. His assurances made me proud, and I settled in with my family and waited.

A few hours before dawn, the whistling winds grew in volume. I turned on the radio, hoping to pick up an AM channel in South Carolina to get local reports. I did, but station after station went off the air as the storm marched toward Charlotte. One by one, the Charlotte area stations left the airwaves too. Then our power went out.

When the first light of dawn turned the black night sky violet, I ventured beyond Janice's protestations to look out through our living room windows. What I saw shocked me—tall hardwoods whipping around like bamboo fishing poles, lightning strikes like strobe lights, the horizon pulsing green flashes of exploding electrical transformers. I shivered and hustled back to my family to ride out the storm.

◆　◆　◆

Ninety minutes later, we emerged into an emerald world of downed trees and limbs, and every surface was coated with wet green leaves. After hoisting limbs off my car and sawing through a tree trunk blocking my driveway, I headed to the hospital. My normal ten-minute drive took over forty minutes of detours, backtracks, cutting limbs, and driving through lawns.

At the hospital, things were unexpectedly calm. The disaster plan was active, emergency generators were functioning, and ample volunteer staff and doctors had arrived throughout the night. The emergency room was awaiting mass casualties, but only a trickle of patients had arrived.

In the corridor I saw a teenage boy standing alone, draped in a blanket that hung to his bare knees above his flip-flops. Anxiety and concern flitted across his face. I asked the head nurse about him.

"That sixteen-year-old brought his mother here. A tree fell through their house. He pulled her out from under the limbs that had pinned her to her bed, picked her up, and drove her here at the height of the storm. He carried her in his arms like a baby. She's going to be OK."

"Were his clothes ruined?" I asked, thinking they might have been bloody.

"No. That's the thing. He didn't seem to know that he was wearing just his underwear until he handed his mother to us."

I must have looked concerned, thinking that we ought to be doing more for that son, because the nurse said, "I can read your mind. Don't worry. We've already given him scrubs to wear. But he hasn't taken the time to put them on. His heart is still on his mom. That mother's son is our hero."

Life Lessons

- Pay attention to the weather forecast.
- A young son's love for his mother is an awesome thing to behold.

ROAD RAGE

On September 14, 2016, while driving home from my office in Atlanta, focused on merging into traffic on Interstate 75, a sonic boom exploded behind my head.

I ducked and hunched my shoulders in protective reflex, gripping the steering wheel and bracing for whatever came next.

What just happened?

I hadn't hit the braking car in front of me or anything else that I could tell. I was still rolling along, so it wasn't a blown-out tire. I focused on easing off the road and onto the right shoulder. I knew I needed to stop, but not in the middle of the bridge over the Chattahoochee River. Toward the other side, I crept along.

Through the loud buzzing in my ears, I heard a tinkling sound in the back seat.

Glass. Broken glass sounded like that.

I glanced back over my left shoulder. The backseat side window was missing. I looked over my right shoulder and saw glass covering the back seat. The passenger side backseat window was mostly intact, but in the upper left corner was a hole out with radiating spiderweb cracks, the kind a bullet would make.

Was my car shot?

On the other side of the bridge, I pulled over and tried to call 911. For a couple of minutes, I couldn't figure out how to work my mobile phone. When a 911 operator answered, I told her my car had been shot and wondered if someone was hunting or practice-shooting in the Chattahoochee National Recreation Area. It must have been a stray bullet. It wasn't like anyone had been shooting at *me*—right?

◆ ◆ ◆

Within minutes, blue flashing lights pulled up behind my car and a Georgia state trooper was standing beside my window. I rolled it down.

"Are you injured, sir?" he asked.

"I don't think so."

"Can you get out of your car? Let's step over behind the guardrail where it's more protected."

That's smart, I thought. There were six lanes of southbound traffic roaring by. More sirens approached.

He helped me over the guardrail and asked, "Sir, do you feel pain anywhere?"

"No."

"Do you feel wetness anywhere?"

He's asking if I wet my pants.

The patrolman said, "Sometimes the shock of injury numbs your ability to feel a wound."

Am I in shock?

"No wetness. I don't feel any."

"Sir, can you lift your arms and turn around slowly, so I can see if you are injured and don't know it?"

I managed to do what he asked.

"Do you know what happened?"

I shared my speculation about a random shot from the woods. More cop cars were arriving. And a fire truck. Ambulances. I told him I saw a car pull over up the hill. Now a woman was standing next to her car, looking our way; maybe she saw something.

As two EMTs, a male and female, were crossing the guardrail, the officer said, "I'm going to leave you in the hands of these pros and go find out what that woman knows."

The EMTs asked me all kinds of questions, including if I wanted to go to the hospital and get checked out. I declined. They asked what happened, and I answered as best I could.

The male EMT went to examine my car. He came back and said, "I found an inch indentation in the metal above the rear wheel. That's the strongest part of the car, where a lot of metal meets. A bullet hit there and didn't go through. Probably means it was a low caliber. A second bullet took out both your backseat windows."

Two shots?

The state trooper returned and said, "The woman had been two cars behind you. She saw lots of brake lights, and then the car in front of her swerved around yours on the left. She saw a silver car, then a silver gun in the hand of the driver, reaching across to stick his gun out of the passenger window. Two shots. She didn't get the license tag number, nor the make and model. Nothing else. She and dozens of others called 911 to report a shooting."

I was shot at on purpose. Why? What had I done to get shot at?

By then, the highway was full of flashing lights. I counted twelve cop cars, three firetrucks, five ambulances, and two helicopters overhead. I learned that because

my car was shot in Cobb County, drove onto the interstate, and came to a stop in Fulton County, three jurisdic-
tions were involved. Since the shooting occurred in Cobb
County, they took over.

For a Cobb County detective, a tall man in a black
blazer, I answered the same questions, adding what was
coming back to me. I had been at a stoplight where two
lanes had to make a left turn down the entrance ramp to
the freeway. I was in the left lane, not paying attention (I
didn't tell him I was texting), when the light turned green.
I might have heard a car honk. The car that had been next
to me on my right at the light was already several car
lengths ahead. Picking up speed, we had to merge into one
lane. I decided to pull behind that lead car, but as I did, for
some reason, it braked and slowed way down, making me
brake too. All my attention was toward the right, trying
to merge and not hit that car. Then came the explosion. I
didn't know my car was shot. I didn't see anything on my
left. I never saw the shooter, not even his car.

"Do you remember anything else?" the detective said
more than once.

"I'm trying to think what I did to cause this," I said.

"Listen to me," the detective said. "You did nothing to
deserve this. I don't care what you did; you didn't do anything that justified getting shot. Get that out of your mind."

The detective wrote something down on his pad and
said he was going back to the scene of the shooting to look
for shell casings. He told me the cameras near the stoplight
were for signal control only and did not record anything.
He left me with two remaining paramedics. All the other
responders had left, save for a couple of TV camera crews.

I decided to walk up the hill and thank the lady who
had stopped. She was still talking to a couple of officers.

The paramedics said they would watch me. When I reached her, I looked into her sweet, round, Black face and said, "Thank you for stopping and sharing what you saw."

She smiled at me and said, "I'm just glad you are OK."

I wanted to hug her.

I strolled back to my car, where the paramedics asked me again if I was sure I didn't want to go to the hospital and get checked out.

"Tell you what," I said. "I can tell I'm still pretty upset. How about checking my blood pressure just for kicks?"

The female EMT sat me on the guardrail, attached a blood pressure cuff, and watched her laptop. The cuff tightened three times. She took it off and said, "Mr. Howerton, did you forget to take your blood pressure medicine today?"

"I don't take high blood pressure medicine."

"Well, I've taken it three times, and you're sitting on 214 over 103."

Before I could say "dang," the other paramedic said, "I was an army medic in Iraq, and that reading is quite normal for what you've been through. You have been telling the same story for an hour now. You are not slurring your words. You are acting normal. I suggest you go home and open a bottle of wine."

The detective returned with no more news. He gave me his card and left after helping me knock the remaining window glass out of both backseat windows so my car wouldn't rain glass on the highway during my drive home. He assured me he would let me know if there was anything to report.

I never heard from him again.

I went home alone; Janice was in Wilson, planning her mother's ninety-fifth birthday party. I vacuumed out the glass from my car. Making calls and taking them from loved ones and colleagues, I drank wine until a green bottle of California chardonnay was empty. Doctor's orders.

◆ ◆ ◆

Over the next few days, I heard from well-wishers and retold my story dozens of times. My heart was touched by the expressions of concern from family, coworkers, ministers, church members, and strangers who'd heard my story. I learned that road rage shootings happen more often than one might think. People told me some gangs require a random shooting as initiation. I got another car, never wanting to drive that one again. I only wish I could have reached out to the woman behind me in traffic that day to thank her again for her kindness, but I didn't think to ask her for her information.

A week later, I went to Lassiter's Tavern for supper. I sat at the bar, and one of the female bartenders came over, looking concerned. She asked, "Aren't you the guy I saw on TV last week who was shot at on the interstate?"

I told her that was me.

"I am *so* sorry. Everything is on the house for you tonight, hon."

Four years later, I am wrestling still with what I learned from being a victim of road rage.

Life Lessons
- The next time you get angry at another driver, remember that driver may be angrier. And they may have a gun.
- Always get the names of people who help you if you can. You may want to thank them again someday.

MOON TAG

After Blacksburg beat Giles in football, eight members of my high school team slept over at my house. My parents and sisters were away. Thanks to our team's pledge to each other not to drink until the season's end, zero alcohol was consumed that night. Not one drop, nor any other hallucinogen you might wonder about as this tale unfolds.

Our winning record riled us up to a previously unattained level of macho giddiness. A simple card game of Old Maid morphed into an indoor version of smear ball. Whoever got stuck with the queen of hearts suffered under a pile of bodies raining fists, pinches, tickles, and goosing until he cried uncle—all in good, clean fun, of course.

To this day, none of us remembers who invented the next game that arose out of our testosteronal groupthink. As if from above, the game descended upon us and became known as moon tag. The object of moon tag was to score points by either surprising your opponents by mooning them or catching them before they could get their pants down to moon you.

A game of cat-and-mouse tag by the headlights of dueling Volkswagen Beetles unfolded. One VW took off; thirty seconds later, the other followed. If the headlights of the chasing VW shone on the other VW before its occupants got out and mooned, a point to the chasing team. But if the lead VW got into a spot where its occupants could get out and in position to moon the other when the chaser's headlights hit them, a point for the lead car. Points were not given for mooning any other vehicle—especially not a cop car. So went our creative frivolity, round after round of chase and illuminate; light their car up before they lit you up with cheeky exposures.

An hour or so into this inventive competition, the leading Volkswagen positioned itself in a dark alley. All four occupants were out and in scoring position when the lights of yet another Volkswagen turned into the alley, all of which I saw through the windshield of my chasing Volkswagen. By the time I got my VW into the alley, we saw four moons, two VWs, and a man—Charley Patterson's father—getting out of his VW Beetle.

Charley's dad beheld four illuminated behinds aimed right at him. Then he managed to ask in his serious-father voice, "Charley, is that you?" just before his gut-busting guffaw. He told Charley that he would assure his wife, Lois, that their eldest son was just fine since Charley had failed to let them know he was sleeping over at my house.

After several failed attempts at stifling his laughter, Charley's father said, "You boys, be more careful, now. You hear?" Then he folded himself into his Beetle and drove away.

We slept until noon the next day.

Life Lessons
- "Blinded by the light" can have many meanings.
- It's good to have a father with a sense of humor.

MY FIRST BROTHER AND SISTER

I have vivid memories of the starry night when Dad took me on a long, facts-of-life walk. I was nine years old.

It had been a traumatic day. My dog, Poochie, went into heat, and a pack of canine suitors descended upon her and did what male dogs do. When one got stuck to Poochie end-to-end, I was horrified. I tried to separate them by spraying the offending beast with cold water from our garden hose. During his talk, Dad was kind and factual, explaining what and why things happened to Poochie that day.

Then he turned to human reproduction. He relayed facts and spoke about the miracles of love and sex and children as God's gifts to husbands and wives. To his great credit, Dad tolerated my incredulous questions like, "How often did you have to do *that?*"

I am certain that my father intended to convey that I was a singular gift of God's creation by explaining that while women have one egg, men have millions of sperm, of which one of those millions got to Mom's egg first in an exact instant. Dad declared that I was "a one-of-a-kind, wonderful creation at a unique point in time." I may not have understood everything, but my young brain got the gist of what he was telling me: I was special.

◆ ◆ ◆

Dad did make me feel special that night. But as days passed, I began thinking about that night I was conceived. If Dad's shoelace had broken earlier in the day and shifted the sequence of events by a few seconds so that a different sperm made contact first, then unique me would not exist.

As a middle child, I assumed that I was my parents' second-born until Mom told me that her first two children, a boy and a girl, were born prematurely with underdeveloped lungs, lived a day or two, and died. Mom delivered this news when I was a teenager old enough to learn that she had taken a drug, DES, to help her carry my sisters and me to full term. But DES was no longer prescribed because it caused complications, including cancer, and I needed to know it was a part of my medical history.

"I don't regret taking that drug," Mom said. "If I hadn't taken it, I wouldn't have had you."

I felt loved, wanted, and lucky.

Months later, guilt crept into my consciousness about feeling fortunate that my first brother and sister had died, because Mom and Dad always told me they wanted only three children. Mom never said, "If my first two children had lived, I wouldn't have had you." But she could have.

Not long after Mom's DES revelation, my Exploring post made a field trip to the laboratory of Dr. Leon Arp, an engineering professor at Virginia Tech who had been instrumental in developing infant respirators. Beholding his electromechanical creation that helped countless premature infants survive warmed my heart. Hearing Dr.

Arp speak, I imagined my parents' torment about losing their first two children who could have been saved by his invention. *If this equipment existed then, would I have been born?* My guilt returned.

◆　◆　◆

When I was about forty-five, I drove to Maplewood Cemetery in Durham, North Carolina, to visit the graves of my Howerton ancestors. After misty-eyed visits to the graves of my father, grandfather, and grandmother, cemetery attendants led me to an older Howerton family plot that I had never seen before. In that section of the cemetery, green grass gave way to a blanket of brown leaves dropped from the limbs of random trees. There, I found the headstones of my great-grandfather (my namesake), my great-grandmother, and several great-aunts and uncles, a couple of whom had died in childhood.

I hadn't expected to see several small stones no bigger than a shoebox etched with "Infant Boy Howerton" or "Baby Girl Howerton" and dates that told me they had been conceived by three generations. When I saw two of them dated in the late 1940s, it dawned on me that I could be looking at the graves of my older brother and sister. Tears trailed down my cheeks.

Whenever Mom heard someone say that the loss of a child was "God's plan," she bristled. She considered it especially cruel when someone tried to comfort a grieving parent by saying that God needed a child in heaven more than on earth. "I will never believe that *my* God wanted my child or any young child to die," she would say.

I cannot remember Dad and me talking about his first two children. I know that Dad was first hospitalized for depression in the late 1940s.

◆ ◆ ◆

Since that trip to Maplewood, I have often thought about my first brother and sister. By some cosmic wonder, I feel closer to them.

My existential questions persist. Will I ever meet my first brother and sister? If they had to die for me to exist, should I be thankful for their deaths? Did my first brother and sister have souls? If they had souls, what happened to those souls? Are the souls of children who die in infancy transferred to other children? Do souls "grow" through reincarnation in other bodies? Is this life all there is, or is there "one more," like Ora and Mom used to say? Or are there many more lives? Which religion created by humans is most true to our Creator's cosmic intent? Is life random or part of a master plan? Is the Creator of this of this universe or the same Creator for multiverses? Is a single human life a planned divine act or the result of a random roll of circumstantial chemical dice? Did Neanderthals have souls? You know—simple questions like that.

In his last sermon to our church in Atlanta, the late theologian David Bartlett said that he had an answer to all those sorts of questions. The congregation fell silent and waited through a reverent pause for his voice to boom, "I don't know!"

Now that was something I could believe.

Life Lessons
- That you are the result of so many exact instants in time is an awesome thing to ponder.
- Life is always a miracle, even if science finds a way to explain it someday.

ADVENT IN THE YEAR OF COVID-19

Sandwiched between the 2019 impeachment and elections came zoonotic COVID-19, "novel" to describe not a book but a never-seen-before coronavirus, so titled for its crown of spikes that connect to healthy cells. The pandemic meant stay at home, WHO and CDC guidelines, lockdowns, essential workers, disinfectant wipes, work and learn from home, Zoom meetings, hotspots, toilet paper shortages, hand sanitizer, shelter in place, PPE, ventilators, testing, anosmia and ageusia symptoms, oximeters, and first responder and frontline workers who awed us with their daily, essential-worker heroism. Asynchronous school was born. The isolation of the dying broke our hearts.

Amid this world contagion came videos of brutality, needless death, and proclamations that Black Lives Matter because all lives are supposed to matter, prompting protests, counterprotests, Juneteenth recognition, calls for calm, and law and order. Our rights evoked Shakespearean rifts—to mask or not to mask, that was the necessity and/or exaggeration to opposing minds. Politicians debated science with scientists, for God's sake. Absentee and early voting soared. A record turnout with paralleled spikes—that prickly word again—in cases, hospitalizations, and deaths. States swung with the counts and were called and/or contested. Debates about the merit or curse of our Electoral College returned like a quadrennial comet. Some worried that our tradition of peaceful transition of power was at risk. Now, with vaccines seen as the light at the end of our tunnel, wouldn't it be an ironic tragedy if immunizations on the horizon make us careless too soon? "But we are exhausted and want to get back to normal" is just as true as "the virus doesn't care." We welcomed words of another holiday season: Peace on Earth, noel, Immanuel, good will toward everyone, gifts to others as acts of caring and love, and "I'll be home for Christmas—if only in my dreams."

A New Year beckoned, one in which we hope to push back the virus with miracle vaccines, adapt, and witness pent-up memorial services for friends and loved ones, where we may once again offer gentle touches and strong hugs to accompany our expressions of love and thanks for lives lived abundantly.

At the time of this writing in early 2022, people are still debating science by invoking their beliefs, suspicions, my facts versus your facts, or playing follow the leader. Truth is not beheld as an absolute consensus of learned minds. An ultimate arbiter of truth seems as remote as scientific evidence was in the ancient Greek temple of the Oracle of Delphi. Some people consider the entire COVID-19 pandemic a hoax, even as the variants wreak havoc throughout the world. Some of them learn that a variant is a mutation while doubting the existence of evolution, ignoring that the mere presence of a mutation proves evolution exists.

Personal beliefs and ignorance have distorted the clear ring of truth. Cognitive dissonance reigns over us as we believe conflicting "facts." Motivated reasoning drives us to select facts that prove our preconceived beliefs. How can science, which changes as new facts are discovered and "old facts" are discarded, be heard, understood, accepted, and taught to such minds? The power of emotion over humans making decisions is vastly underestimated and misunderstood.

I used to think the best way to teach humans was by engaging their minds, but now I am beginning to understand how important an open heart is to open minds. One way to open a heart is to show respect for people's opinions by listening to them and understanding why they think or feel that way. Granted, that can be arduous work, especially if their "facts" sound to you like they could be howled at the moon.

But I've come to learn that the best way to get people to listen is to listen to them first. After all, it's hard to expect someone to care what you think until they think you care about them.

Life Lessons
- Some people don't make sense to you and never will. Listen to them anyway. Love them anyway.
- Mutations prove evolution.

MY DREAM WITHIN A DREAM

I am being chased down a wide corridor. Everything is gray and bare. There is nowhere to hide. They are catching up with me.

I squat down along the edge of the wall and try to make myself small, waiting for the inevitable, the crush of whatever comes next.

Somehow, I know it's not me who is being chased. It is Jesus Christ. I don't know how I know, but I do. The mob is driving Jesus to the hill called Calvary.

I hunker down, lowering my face so that no one will recognize me. They pass, and all goes quiet.

I lift my eyes in the direction they went. And there, not fifteen feet away, I see Jesus on his cross, his head hanging down. Just me and Jesus, no one else.

Jesus raises his head slowly. He turns his battered face to look at me. Our eyes lock. And then, Jesus winks . . . and smiles.

"Wake up! Wake up!" a girl's voice says.

◆ ◆ ◆

I am sleeping on a floor. I open my eyes and see a young girl, maybe seven or eight, standing over me. She is wearing a white shirt dress.

"Come with me," she says. Then, she turns and leaves through an open doorway, expecting me to follow.

I get up off the hard-packed earth and walk out of a straw-and-timber hut and into a village, where people do morning things like medieval peasants might do. The girl is ahead, walking toward a forest. I follow her, trying to catch up.

We walk into the forest until it opens onto a flat field of green grass, where five young men are running in a circle. They are wearing sky-blue basketball uniforms and struggling with each other as they circle the same spot. Closer now, I see that a delicate silver chain binds them together. Their uniforms say "Old Dominion" in white letters. They are all white men with dark hair.

The young girl turns to me. She points toward them and says, "Help them. You must help them!"

I wake up.

◆ ◆ ◆

I have never had any dream like this one before or since, nor have I had another dream within a dream. I have never dreamed about faith or religion before or since. Jesus Christ has appeared to me only this once in this dream.

This dream is the only dream that I have remembered in detail since the night it came to me. I was in my early forties and struggling with what I believed; my doubts about my faith tormented me. In the months that followed, I shared this dream with Janice, my father, a few close friends, several ministers, mentors, and, years later, adults in a church gathering. And now with you.

Over the years, I have come to see this dream as a great gift. I have come to believe that Jesus Christ's smile was and is a blessing, allowing me to forgive myself for doubting so much, as if to give myself a spiritual break. Frederick Buechner's writing, "Doubt is the ants in the pants of faith," has enlightened and comforted me. I have quoted him many times, amending his words to "of a *growing* faith" more than once. My faith has grown since I embraced my doubts. Stiff-arming my doubts only fed my stagnating guilt.

When asked about the little girl, I can only say that she was no one I recognized and someone I trusted and knew I had to follow.

The Old Dominion basketball players are puzzling. I grew up in the state of Virginia, which is nicknamed Old Dominion. The Old Testament book of Genesis says that God blessed Adam and Eve saying they should "have dominion over . . . all living things." That the young men were tied together by a delicate silver chain, one that they could easily break, might suggest how we are burdened spiritually by old, weak thinking and beliefs, and by paternalism from which we could unbind ourselves and run free in God's creation.

But who knows?

Life Lessons
- Some dreams might speak to your heart, mind, and spirit.
- You might be surprised how much your faith will grow if you embrace your doubts.

KHRUSHCHEV, KENNEDY, AND STING

Before the measles vaccine came along, I suffered through that invasion of red spots and high fever like most kids my age. My measles coincided with the end of second grade, postponing the advent of my carefree summer. Mom confined me to bed and told me to be still and quiet as possible.

One afternoon, my older sister, Carol, came in and sat on the edge of my bed. She was crying. I asked her what was wrong.

"Nikita Khrushchev just said, 'We will bury you!'"

I asked who he was.

"He's the head of Russia. He wants to kill *all* Americans. To bury us!" She paused and added, "And I'll miss Mama and Daddy so much!" She boo-hooed, and I started crying because I would miss Mom and Dad too.

"But why?" I asked.

"I don't know. He just does."

Carol left me feeling hopeless. My measles lingered for

weeks, but they didn't kill me, and neither did that mean man who wanted to bury me.

◆ ◆ ◆

Three years later, in October of 1962, I was huddling under my desktop in my sixth-grade classroom practicing nuclear war safety drills as if the slab of wood over my head would offer protection against an atomic bomb. Khrushchev was still at it, but now we had President Kennedy issuing counterthreats in a dance of pending destruction in what is now known as the Cuban Missile Crisis. It was surreal to see adults crying as we watched public service announcements on TV in which cartoon characters taught us how to maximize our chances of surviving nuclear fallout, as if we could survive the initial megaton blasts. Luckily, no bluffs were called, and the two leaders backed down. Our history says Kennedy made Khrushchev cave; Russian history probably says something else.

◆ ◆ ◆

Years later, I learned about nuclear deterrence theory. It dawned on me that the future existence of the human race rested on threats of don't-do-that-because-we'll-do-it-back-to-you-only-worse and was highly dependent upon the caliber of mental calculus of sworn enemies. A fragile peace. But threats and counterthreats of our missiles against your missiles somehow kept nuclear war at bay.

◆ ◆ ◆

After more years ticked away, I became a father of three sons. One day, I heard Sting singing on the radio that "Russians love their children too." Listening to Sting's haunting song tucked me back in my old measles bed with Khrushchev.

But somewhere amid the song's ponderous Slavic instrumental hook, an epiphany settled over me as I began to contemplate that our survival of the Cold War may have been because of something far more powerful than logic or rational strategy. Oh, sure, our leaders could have wiped out both of our countries, whether by calculated intent, political illogic, immature bravado, or an unintended cascade of concurrent errors. And, of course, diplomacy and weapon effectiveness were and are important to preserving long-term deterrence. But could it be that our existence rested just as much on the reality that we both love our children? Was it that reality of sweet parental love for current and future generations that pushes us off the edge of annihilation?

As new nuclear powers emerge on our beloved Earth, and we seek diplomatic and deterrent solutions, let us hope and pray that those leaders love their children too.

Life Lessons
- It's tough to learn about the end of the world when you are a sick child. It doesn't get much easier as an adult.
- Parents should talk to kids about current events. They take in more than you might think.

OUTRUNNING A STORM

One summer day in 1962 found Mom, Dad, my sisters, and me crossing Montana, homeward bound in our Oldsmobile 98 sedan, jam-packed with camping gear and luggage for our ten-thousand-mile road trip. Having departed the sublime beauty of Glacier National Park, we drove east. We stopped for lunch at a hamburger joint, part of a new chain apparently named after some Scot who was fond of giant arcs of yellow neon. After spending less than three bucks feeding our clan, we discovered a fierce thunderstorm was blowing in. We ran for the car (there was no inside seating) and drove out from under the pelting rain until we were back in the sunshine.

This was before weather channels and smartphones with radar apps, and Dad had never driven faster along the two-lane highway with no speed limit, keeping us ahead of the storm as we crossed grassy plains. But the tempest trailed us with an ominous constancy. We were barely keeping our distance when our left rear tire blew out.

We pulled off into the grass and Dad and I raced to dig through our stuffed trunk for the jack and spare tire.

Just when we got the car jacked up and the lug nuts loosened, hail pelted us in sideways sheets of rain.

"Get back in the car!" Dad yelled, and there we sat in solemn silence, watching the mothballs of ice turn the fields around us white. When our trunk lid blew open, we knew everything in it was getting soaked. The sound of breaking glass told us our Coleman lantern had taken a direct hit.

I sat among my family, none of us uttering a word. The incessant pounding the hail was giving our roof would have deafened our words if we'd tried.

And just like that, the hail stopped, and the rain slowed to a dribble. Rays of sunlight broke through, low in the western sky behind us.

Dad and I got out of the car, and as we did, against a wall of black clouds moving toward the east, a full rainbow appeared.

It remains the most beautiful rainbow I have ever seen.

Life Lessons
- Sometimes it's best to turn and face the storm, let it pass over you, and see the rainbow on the other side.
- It's hard to outrun Mother Nature.

CONCLUSION

Throughout this book, I've shared stories that have taught me important lessons or brought my family together. I sincerely hope I've inspired you to laugh, think, or at least shake your head at our antics and misadventures.

Now, it's your turn.

I'd like to invite you to tell your own stories and life lessons that the story might have prompted you to recall. No matter who you are, you have stories that someone wants and needs to hear. Please don't let your stories die with you. Let them out to live another day. Share them with your friends, your family; it will strengthen your connections and bring you closer than ever. Share them with strangers; you never know what effect you might have and whom you might end up calling a friend. People will remember the stories you tell and thank you for telling them. And they will benefit from what you've experienced and learned along the journey we call life.

Stories are an act of sharing, and this book is just words on a page unless I know that I've connected with someone. To ask a question, share what lessons you've learned, or tell me your own stories, reach out at www.richardhowerton.com.

Thank you for reading, and thank you for sharing your stories.

APPENDIX A: LOCATIONS

The stories in this book have taken place in various and wide-ranging parts of our wonderful world, from Beijing to Burlington to my very own backyard. For your convenience, I offer this list of stories grouped by location, each of which holds its own special place in my heart, mind, and soul.

Cambria, CA
Didn't You See Me? 155.

Charlotte, NC
A Hugo Mother's Son 243.
A Secondary Emotion 72.
DMV Photo 206.
Flying with a Mortician 221.
Follow Your Bliss 135.
"Forked" 30.
I Didn't Even Know You Were
  Pregnant! 6.
Joey's Tooth 232.
Marshall 116.
My Dream within a Dream 261.
Roy Rogers and Me 32.
The Colossus of Another Rhodes
  87.
Time Management Priority 57.
Wrong Blood Tragedy 118.

Chesapeake, VA
Cat Scratch Fever 92.
Roto-Rooter Man 215.

Chicago, IL
Tummy Tickle 52.
The Brady Bunch 198.

Cody, WY
Cowboys and Indians 112.

Durham, NC
Haircut Surprise 173.
My First Brother and Sister 254.

Florence, Italy
Love in Florence 75.

Glacier National Park, MT
Waking Up Next to a Brand-New
  Something 46.

Hong Kong, China
The Great Walls of China 16.

Indianapolis, IN
Hail the Queen 101.

Las Vegas, NV
Airport Boot 182.
Ralph's Rattlesnake Ranch 217.

Lexington, VA
Lexington Revisited 234.

Lincolnton, NC
Roy Rogers and Me 32.

London, England
Uninvited Riders 54.

Los Angeles, CA
Gulf Station Sleepover 146.

Luxembourg City,
  Luxembourg
British Schoolboys 41.

Mohave Desert, CA
Charlie's Radiator Shop 19.
Ralph's Rattlesnake Ranch 217.

Morehead City, NC
Your Son Is Fine, But . . . 168.

Montana
Outrunning a Storm 267.

APPENDIX A: LOCATIONS

Mount Airy, NC
A Yoke of Justice 158.
Dad's Illness: Part IV 165.
Hole in the Water 10.
Ora and the Snake 184.
Living in a Parsonage 175.
This Life and One More 240.

New York, NY
Angel on Fifth Avenue 97.
Dad's Illness: Part V 202.
Fainting in the Holland Tunnel
25.
Nice, Nice, Very Nice 176.

Oxford, NC
Fighting to Care 160.
Size Small 211.
Only One Cowboy 213.

Paris, France
Paris Riot 64.
The Folies Bergère 90.

Portsmouth, VA
Flush Water Planning 207.
Power Outage 35.
Will You See Me Now? 144.
The Elizabeth River 178.

Reims, France
Sick in Reims 70.

Rome, Italy
Lost in Rome 81.

San Francisco, CA
Bible Convention 189.

Shanghai, China
Business with People You Know
194.
Lost in Translation 43.

Wilson, NC
Get Down 133.
Cincinnati 110.

Winston-Salem, NC
Dad's Illness: Part V 202.
Intoxicant Love 139.
Advent in the First Year of
COVID-19 258.
The Power of Goals 153.
Uncle Tebo's Advice 84.

Yellowstone National Park,
WY
Do You See Any Wildlife? 4.

APPENDIX B: THEMES

If you are looking for a story relative to a specific topic or theme, I offer these broad categories to assist you, knowing these stories could fall into many other areas of interest as well.

Road Trips and Family Vacations

Help in Unexpected Places

Grief and Loss

APPENDIX B: THEMES

ABOUT THE AUTHOR

Richard Howerton has been a preacher's kid, lawn boy, carpet cleaner, moving man, high school football player, telephone installer/repairman, real estate perc tester and lumberjack, quarry stone and asphalt weigher, construction worker, waiter, office worker, naval officer, hospital administrator, health system executive, Sunday school teacher, film critic, and writer. He married his college sweetheart, Janice Pope, with whom he now approaches a golden anniversary celebration with their three sons, two daughters-in-law, and four grandkids. A native of Lincolnton, North Carolina, Richard was raised in Blacksburg, Virginia. He and Janice have resided in Mount Airy, North Carolina; Durham, North Carolina; Chesapeake, Virginia; Oxford, North Carolina; Burlington, North Carolina; Charlotte, North Carolina; and Atlanta, Georgia. He majored in politics at Wake Forest University and holds a master's degree in health administration from Duke University. He and Janice now reside in the wonderful city of Winston-Salem, North Carolina.

www.ingramcontent.com/pod-product-compliance
Lightning Source LLC
Chambersburg PA
CBHW062321120626
46553CB00015B/181